Return Migration, Health, and Sexuality in a Transnational Mexican Community

Migración de Retorno, Salud y Sexualidad en una Comunidad Mexicana Transnacional

I0417098

edited by

Wayne A. Cornelius
Alejandra Lizardi-Gómez
Allison Van Vooren
David Keyes

Center For Comparative Immigration Studies
University Of California, San Diego

Centro Universitario Del Norte
Universidad De Guadalajara

La Jolla, California
Colotlán, Jalisco

RETURN MIGRATION, HEALTH, AND SEXUALITY IN A TRANSNATIONAL MEXICAN COMMUNITY
MIGRACIÓN DE RETORNO, SALUD Y SEXUALIDAD EN UNA COMUNIDAD MEXICANA TRANSNACIONAL

edited by
Wayne A. Cornelius, Alejandra Lizardi-Gómez, Allison Van Vooren, David Keyes

D.R. © 2013 Primera Edición, 2013, Guadalajara, Jalisco, México.

ISBN: 978-1497373549

Diseño y Diagramación en Prometeo Editores por
Jorge Carlos De la Torre Guzmán

Impresión
Prometeo Editores S.A. de C.V.
Libertad 1457, Col. Americana.
C.P. 44160 Guadalajara, Jalisco, México.
Tels: 3826 2726 y 3826 2782

Center for Comparative Immigration Studies
University of California, San Diego
9500 Gilman Drive
La Jolla, California 92093

Centro Universitario del Norte
Universidad de Guadalajara
Carretera Federal No. 23, Km. 191
Colotlán, Jalisco, C.P. 46200

Cover Photography by Alison Van Vooren | Cover Design by Bret Silvis

Este libro se publicó con el apoyo del Programa Integral de Fortalecimiento Institucional, PIFI 2013.

CONTENTS
ÍNDICE

Tlacuitapa, Jalisco, central plaza. (Photo by Risa Farrell)

1   Introduction

Wayne A. Cornelius, Alejandra Lizardi-Gómez,
Allison Van Vooren

This book reports on research conducted in 2012-13 by the Mexican Migration Field Research and Training Program (MMFRP), based in the center for Comparative Immigration Studies at the University of California, San Diego. Established in 2004, the MMFRP seeks to train a new generation of students to become proficient field researchers in international migration studies. An additional goal each year is to create a new, individual-level database on Mexican migration that can be used to address key issues of public policy on both sides of the border. The MMFRP's field research sites as well as the substantive foci vary from year to year.

One of the program's principal research sites is Tlacuitapa, Jalisco, a town whose four generations of migrants to the United States have formed satellite communities in Union City, California and Oklahoma City, Oklahoma. First studied by a research team led by Wayne Cornelius in 1976, Tlacuitapa has been the site of MMFRP fieldwork in 2005, 2007, 2010, and 2013. This body of research has explored a broad range of issues affecting migrants and the relatives they leave behind, including the dynamics of migration decision-making and U.S. settlement behavior, labor market participation, remittance flows, education, nutritional changes, reproductive health, cultural changes, and the effects of various U.S. immigration laws and policies on the ways in which Tlacuitapenses manage their livelihoods (see Cornelius and Lewis, 2007; Cornelius, Fitzgerald and Borger, 2009; and Fitzgerald, Alarcón, and Muse-Orlinoff, 2011).

These issues are hardly unique to Tlacuitapa. They broadly characterize other high-emigration communities in Mexico, especially those with a multi-generational tradition of U.S.-bound migration. What makes our most recent field research among Tlacuitapenses unique is that it is part of a sustained effort to document social, economic, and policy-related phenomena occurring in a specific migrant-sending community and its U.S. expatriate communities over a period of nearly four decades, using a multidisciplinary, binational approach.

The MMFRP's 2012-13 project explored several key migration and health phenomena affecting Tlacuitapa and its migrants at the time of our fieldwork (January-March 2013). While previous research had examined the effects of the 2007-09 economic crisis on migration to the United States, the 2012-13 study focused on how the crisis had affected return migration from the United States to Tlacuitapa and decisions to settle indefinitely in the United States. MMFRP researchers also studied Tlacuitapenses' knowledge of, and participation in, the Deferred Action for Childhood Arrivals (DACA) program, an Obama administration initiative launched in 2012 that gives qualified, young undocumented immigrants the opportunity to seek temporary relief from deportation (Chapter 2). The team's investigation of health-related issues devoted special attention to access to health services on both sides of the border (Chapter 3), chronic disease management (Chapter 4), workplace health hazards (Chapter 5), and the perception and social construction of HIV risk (Chapter 6).

MIGRATION FROM TLACUITAPA TO THE UNITED STATES IN THE FIRST DECADE OF THE 21ST CENTURY

Tlacuitapa, part of the Unión de San Antonio municipality in the Los Altos region of Jalisco, has a long history of migration to the United States, beginning in the early 20th century. The most common migration destinations for Tlacuitapenses historically have been in Texas, California, and Oklahoma. In these places and a few other states (Illinois, Michigan, Nevada, Oregon), Tlacuitapenses have constructed extensive social networks, acquired legal residence and naturalized citizenship, and put down solid roots in local labor markets (Cabrera-Hernández, 2011).

In recent years, the profile of migration has changed in Tlacuitapa. Interviews done in 2013 revealed that that the number of new migrants leaving Tlacuitapa had decreased significantly, and that Oklahoma, rather than California, had become the principal destination of choice for first-time migrants. While new departures haven fallen, unauthorized migration to the United States is still occurring, and the eventual success rate among those attempting entry remains high. Among our 2013 interviewees who had been detained on their first attempt at unauthorized border crossing, nearly nine out of ten (86 percent) were able to cross successfully on the second or third try, without returning to Tlacuitapa (see Chapter, 2).

The issue of migrant settlement in the United States has been explored regularly in MMFRP studies since 2004. These studies have found that labor market conditions and border control had shaped U.S. settlement decisions among Tlacuitapenses. Such decisions were frequently an unintended consequence of tightened border enforcement, as well as the result of increased interaction with U.S. society (López, Oliphant, and Tejeda, 2007; Jarvis et al., 2009). MMFRP fieldwork conducted in 2010 explored the impact of the Great Recession on migrant settlement (Bridges, Hong, and Valencia, 2011). MMFRP researchers found that most Tlacuitapenses already living in the United States did not plan to return to Mexico despite the recession, opting to dig in and develop new coping strategies -- reducing the remittances they sent to relatives in Mexico, taking second jobs, engaging in self-employment, etc. -- that enabled them to withstand diminished income (due to fewer working hours) and employment insecurity (Cabrera-Hernández et al., 2011).

Chapter 2 builds on this earlier MMFRP research, exploring the relative importance of economic, policy-related, and social factors in determining decisions to settle in the United States or to return to Mexico, particularly in the context of the economic contraction of 2007-09. The researchers find that policy variables – tougher border enforcement, debates on immigration reform, and the Deferred Action for Childhood Arrivals (DACA) program – had played a relatively insignificant role in these decisions. Rather, economic and social factors were the primary determinants of the decision to settle or return.

Tlacuitapense migrants have been settling in the United States because of perceived improvement in well-being, relatively better employment opportunities (despite the U.S. recession), and long-term prospects for higher earnings. On the other hand, Tlacuitapenses who had returned to Mexico in recent years overwhelmingly cited a decrease in income due to the U.S. economic crisis as their primary reason for returning.

HEALTH CIRCUMSTANCES AND EXPERIENCES OF TLACUITAPENSES

This volume devotes special attention to four major issues in immigrant health: access to health care services on both sides of the border, how chronic diseases like diabetes are managed transnationally, how migration affects workplace-based health hazards, and migration-related factors influencing the risk of acquiring HIV. These issues are of global importance, given the continued increase in international and internal migration movements and the need to build support networks for health care.

In recent years, chronic diseases have surpassed infectious diseases as the primary cause of mortality in both Mexico and the United States (WHO, 2011). Managing chronic disease transnationally requires more intensive use of health care services which, in the context of migration and two dissimilar health care systems, can lead to greater unmet heath needs. Concerning occupational health and safety, the kinds of jobs held by migrants and increasing labor market participation among those who are left behind raise the risk of occupational injury and temporary or permanent disabilities. Regarding HIV, migration increases the risk of HIV transmission due to economic instability, family separation, poor access to care, and proximity to injection drugs and sex workers (Ojeda et al., 2012; Brouwer et al., 2006; Sánchez et al., 2004). Each of these health issues was explored in depth in the MMFRP's 2012-13 study.

In fieldwork conducted in Tlacuitapa in 2005, MMFRP researchers investigated the use of health services as an indicator of migrants' integration into American society. López et al. (2007) found that as Tlacuitapenses become more established in the United States, they are more likely to use health care services there. In addition, migrants whose primary residence remains in Mexico are less likely to use health care services in the United States and often return to their place of origin if they suffer health issues. This study identified the fear of deportation as a key impediment to health care-seeking among undocumented migrants, along with lack of knowledge of the U.S. health care system, language barriers, and discrimination.

Chapter 3 of this volume explores Tlacuitapenses' current perceived barriers to health care. Migrants interviewed in 2013 mentioned fear when accessing health care services due to undocumented status, the cost of services, various forms of discrimination, and language barriers between patients and health care professionals. Specifically, we found that undocumented Tlacuitapenses are less likely to access health care services and more likely to report that fear of revealing their immigration status caused them to avoid or delay care. However, both documented and undocumented migrants encounter significant language barriers when accessing health care and often must provide their own translators. Comparing the two main satellite communities of Tlacuitapenses in the United States, we found that those living in California have better access to care than those in Oklahoma, as measured by having a primary care provider and having accessed health services in the last year. This difference may partly reflect the anti-immigrant measures implemented in Oklahoma during the last decade.

Diabetes has become an increasing public health concern in both the United States and Mexico. In the United States the prevalence of diabetes tripled from 1990 to 2010 (CDC, 2011). The disease is especially widespread among U.S. Latinos, whose prevalence of diabetes is nearly two times that of non-Hispanic whites (CDC, 2012). In 2007, MMFRP researchers studied the medical conditions that create a need for health care services, especially Type 2 diabetes (Oristian et al., 2009). Moreover, Tlacuitapense migrants were found to be more likely than non-migrating residents of the town to report obesity and high cholesterol, two clinical risk factors for diabetes. Additionally, local health professionals in public and private clinics in Tlacuitapa noted the prevalence of diabetes complications as a major reason for medical consults. One of the possible explanations for this finding is changing nutritional practices among migrants faced with sociocultural adaptation challenges in the United States.

Chapter 4 of this volume investigates the social, cultural, and economic determinants of diabetes-related health issues. Specifically, the researchers ask: How do Tlacuitapenses' interactions with formal health systems influence diabetes-related health? What are the physical activity and nutritional practices of people in this transnational community? How do these practices affect diabetes-related health? To understand these dynamics, the authors investigate various matters related to prevention, including information about diabetes, diabetes screening tests, and visits to a clinic or medical facility. To better understand interviewees' nutrition and exercise practices, researchers asked them about the types of food they eat during the day and the amount of physical activity experienced at work, while doing housework, and during recreational activities.

Overall, Tlacuitapense men in particular are more isolated from the health care system in both Mexico and the United States than are women. This significantly affects undocumented male migrants living in the United States, especially when legal status, the disruptive experience of migration, and lower education levels reduce the amount of diabetes-related information they receive. Upon analysis, Tlacuitapense women were found to consume healthier foods than men. In general, however the types of foods consumed by Tlacuitapenses were found to be sub-optimal in preventing diabetes. Currently, there are relatively few preventive and disease management practices in place among Tlacuitapenses on either side of the border.

The 2013 MMFRP project investigated, for the first time in Tlacuitapa, health hazards related to the workplace. Most occupational health studies focus on agricultural work-related injuries (Sakala, 1987; Schenker and McCurdy, 1990; Mobed et al., 1992; Stallones et al., 2009; McCauley et al., 2006). In recent decades, however, construction has surpassed agriculture as the most common U.S. occupation among migrants from Tlacuitapa, allowing us to compare occupational health issues among agricultural and non-agricultural workers.

In Chapter 5 the researchers ask: In which country -- Mexico or the United States -- are Tlacuitapenses safer in regards to occupational health? To explore this question they focus on four key indicators of occupational health: perceived safety in the workplace, workplace abuses or accidents, reported injuries, and medical attention received for accidents. Overall, Tlacuitapenses experience higher rates of workplace injuries in the United States (28 percent) than in Mexico (14.9 percent). Men are more susceptible to occupational injuries in the United States because they overwhelmingly work in construction, the sector with the highest proportion of occupational injuries (78.6 percent). Women living in Tlacuitapa are slightly more susceptible to workplace injuries than female migrants in the United States, as a consequence of the limited employment opportunities available to them -- mainly jobs in a small factory where they are at a particularly high risk for injuries. In both the United States and Mexico, Tlacuitapenses average roughly two work-related injuries throughout their lifetime. Regarding perceptions of workplace hazards, females in Mexico are most likely to recognize dangerous working conditions while males who work in the United States are most likely to think that their employers try to minimize risk, despite the fact that male migrants suffer the highest proportion of work-related injuries. The most common types of workplace abuse in both countries were wage theft (non-payment of wages earned) and verbal abuse. Overall, Tlacuitapenses were found to have relatively poor employment-related health in both Mexico and the United States.

Finally, the latest MMFRP project built on previous MMFRP research on sexual health, which began in 2007 with an analysis of gender dynamics

(Muse-Orlinoff et al., 2009) and continued with a study of condom use in 2010 (Goldenberg, Kessler and Quesada, 2011). In Chapter 6 the authors explore the socially constructed risk of HIV and other sexually transmitted disease among Tlacuitapenses. Research has demonstrated that Mexican migrants to the United States are particularly vulnerable to HIV infection (Hirsch 2009, 2002; Magis-Rodríguez, 2009; Ojeda et al., 2012). Recently, a growing proportion of HIV cases among women in rural Mexico have been linked to male migrants who were infected in the United States and transmitted the infection to their partners upon return (Rangel et al., 2006).

Noting Tlacuitapa's long tradition of migration and the Los Altos region's historically conservative sexual norms, MMFRP researchers investigated the community's attitudes and practices surrounding the use of condoms as a form of HIV prevention. They examine risk behaviors and sexual relationships in a socio-cultural context, taking into account the institutional structures that create and facilitate the risk of acquiring a sexually transmitted illness. Among these structures are a tough U.S. border enforcement regime, which elevates the social status of migrant men who successfully cross the fortified border and/or establish themselves in the United States.

One of the key findings reported in Chapter 6 is the discrepancy between attitudes about condom use and actual sexual health practices. Although respondents recognized the effectiveness of condoms in preventing HIV transmission, reported condom use was relatively low. The authors argue that this disparity between attitudes and practices may be due, in part, to socially conservative norms in Tlacuitapa that discourage pre-marital sex and use rumors to as a form of social control of female virginity. However, Tlacuitapenses living in the United States are generally more in favor of condom use as a socially accepted means of HIV and STI prevention.

METHODOLOGY

The Mexican Migration Field Research and Training Program seeks to document and explain changes in Mexico-to-U.S. migration and U.S. settlement behavior by studying, in great depth, three specific communities with extensive migration histories and their satellite communities of migrants in the United States. Each community is restudied on a three-year cycle. The fieldwork is carried out each year by a team of approximately thirty bilingual students from Mexico and the United States. Student interviewers receive three months of training to conduct standardized survey interviews, ethnographic observation, and qualitative interviews. The MMFRP's principal research sites in Mexico were selected purposively to maximize variation in length of U.S. migration history, ethnic composition (mestizo vs. indigenous), and development/poverty level. Each research site is relatively small, roughly ranging from 1,300 to 2,900 inhabitants.

MMFRP interviewers seek to interview every adult aged 18 to 65 found to be living in the research community (or visiting from the United States) at the time of the fieldwork. Since researchers attempt to interview the entire adult population there is no sampling design and therefore limited sampling error. We do not claim that the resulting data are statistically representative of the entire rural Mexican population nor of all Mexican migrants to the United States. However, the given the social, cultural, and economic diversity among the MMFRP research communities we believe them to be broadly representative of rural, high-emigration communities in Mexico. Among U.S.-based migrants from the Mexican research community a snowball sample is interviewed during the two months immediately following fieldwork in Mexico. Contact information for migrants living in the United States, gathered from interviewees in the sending community, enables interviewers to approach their friends and relatives living in U.S. satellite communities.

The standardized survey questionnaire used in the 2013 study was programmed into electronic tablets. Electronic data capture eliminated most questionnaire administration and data transfer errors. During the training phase of the program, students are encouraged to engage the interviewee conversationally in the interview process while ensuring confidentiality and anonymity. Given the high sensitivity of migration and health topics, MMFRP researchers respect the interviewee's right to refuse to participate or to answer specific questions and are dedicated to a very high standard of research ethics.

ACKNOWLEDGEMENTS

Since 2004 the people of Tlacuitapa, on both sides of the border, have graciously collaborated with MMFRP's ongoing research. We are deeply grateful to them for sharing their life stories and welcoming us so warmly into their homes. We are also indebted to the Ford Foundation, the Center for American Progress, Eleanor Roosevelt College at the University of California-San Diego (UCSD), and UCSD's Vice Chancellor for Equity, Diversity, and Inclusion for their generous financial support of MMFRP, and to the Universidad de Guadalajara for supporting the publication of this book.

REFERENCES

Brouwer, K.C., et al. (2009) Deportation along the U.S.-Mexico Border: Its Relation to Drug Use Patterns and Accessing Care. Journal of Immigrant and Minority Health, 11(1):1-6.

FitzGerald, D.S, Alarcón, R., and Muse-Orlinoff, L., eds.(2011). Recession Without Borders: Mexican Migrants Confront the Economic Downturn. La Jolla, CA: Center for Comparative Immigration Studies, UCSD.

Cabrera-Hernández, J., Hall, A., de Anda J., Romero, D.R., & Saldaña, R. (2011). Coping with Hard Times in El Norte. In D.S . FitzGerald, R. Alarcon, & L. Muse-Orlinoff (eds.), Recession Without Borders: Mexican Migrants Confront the Economic Downturn (95-109). La Jolla, CA: Center for Comparative Immigration Studies, UCSD.

CDC (2011). (Centers for Disease Control and Prevention).. National diabetes fact sheet: national estimates and general information on diabetes and prediabetes in the United States, 2011. Atlanta, GA: U.S. Department of Health and Human Services, Centers for Disease Control and Prevention.

—(2012). (Centers for Disease Control and Prevention). (2012). Diabetes Report Card 2012. Atlanta, GA: Centers for Disease Control and Prevention, U.S. Department of Health and Human Services.

Cornelius, W., FitzGerald D., & Borger, S., eds. (2009) Four Generations of Norteños: New Research from the Cradle of Mexican Migration. La Jolla, CA: Center for Comparative Immigration Studies, UCSD.

Cornelius, W., & Lewis J.M., eds. (2007) Impacts of Border Enforcement on Mexican Migration. The View from Sending Communities. La Jolla, CA: Center for Comparative Immigration Studies, UCSD.

Goldenberg, S., Kessler K, & Quesada L. (2011). Contraceptive Use in a Community of International Migration. In D.S. FitzGerald, R. Alarcon, & L. Muse-Orlinoff (eds.), Recession Without Borders: Mexican Migrants Confront the Economic Downturn (132-152). La Jolla, CA: Center for Comparative Immigration Studies, UCSD.

López, H., Oliphant, R., & Tejeda, E. (2007). U.S. Settlement Behavior and Labor Market Participation. In: W.Cornelius, and J.M. Lewis (eds.) (75-96). Impacts of Border Enforcement on Mexican Migration:The View from Sending Communities. La Jolla, CA: Center for Comparative Immigration Studies, UCSD.

McCauley, A., Langley, K., & Rohlman R. (2006). Studying Health Outcomes in Farmworker Populations Exposed to Pesticides. Environmental Health Perspectives, 114(6): 953-960.

Mobed, K., Gold, E.B. & Schenker, M. (1992). Occupational Health Problems among Migrant and Seasonal Farm Workers. Western Journal of Medicine, 157(3): 367-373.

Muse-Orlinoff, L., Córdova, J., Angulo, L.C., Kanungo, M., & Rodríguez, R. (2009). Families in Transition: Migration and Gender Dynamics in Sending and Receiving Communities. In: Cornelius, W., FitzGerald D., & Borger, S. (eds.) (181-214) Four Generations of Norteños: New Research from the Cradle of Mexican Migration. La Jolla, CA: Center for Comparative Immigration Studies, UCSD.

Ojeda, V.D., Burgos, J.L., Rangel, M.G., Lozada, R., Vera, A. (2012) U.S. Drug Use and Migration Experiences of Mexican Female Sex Workers Who Are Injection Drug Users. Journal of Health Care for the Poor and Underserved, forthcoming.

Sakala, C. (1987). Migrant and Seasonal Farmworkers in the United States: A Review of Health Hazards, Status, and Policy. International Migration Review, 21(3): 659-87.

Rangel, G.M., Martínez-Donate, A.P., Hovell, M.F., Santibáñez, J., Sipan, C.L., & Izazola-Licea, J.A. (2006). Prevalence of risk factors for HIV infection among Mexican migrants and immigrants: probability survey on the northern border of Mexico. Salud Pública de México, 48(1): 3–12. (doi:10.1590/S0036-36342006000100003),

Schenker, M.B., & McCurdy, S.A. (1990). Occupational health among migrant and seasonal farmworkers: the specific case of dermatitis. American Journal of Independent Medicine, 18(3): 345-51.

Stallones, L., Vela Acosta, M.S., Sample, P., Bigelow, P., & Rosales, M. (2009). Perspectives on safety and health among migrant and seasonal farmworkers in the United States and México: a qualitative field study. Journal of Rural Health, 25(2): 219–225.

WHO (World Health Organization). (2011). Noncommunicable diseases country profiles. Geneva: Switzerland.

Introducción

Wayne A. Cornelius, Alejandra Lizardi-Gómez, Allison Van Vooren

La investigación que da lugar a este libro surge del trabajo durante los años 2012 y 2013 del Programa de Trabajo de Campo y Entrenamiento sobre la Migración Mexicana (MMFRP, por sus siglas en inglés) con base en el Centro de Estudios Migratorios Comparados (CCIS, por sus siglas en inglés) en la Universidad de California, San Diego. Este programa se ha llevado a cabo desde el año 2004, con el objeto de enseñar a una nueva generación de estudiantes, a llevar a cabo investigaciones de campo sobre migración internacional. Tiene también una meta adicional, que es generar nuevas bases de datos a nivel individual sobre migración mexicana que puedan ser utilizadas para abordar cuestiones claves de política pública, y desarrollar con ello conciencia pública sobre temas migratorios en Estados Unidos y México.

Los temas de investigación y los lugares de estudio varían año con año. Una de las comunidades binacionales en las que los estudiantes del MMFRP han realizado investigaciones, es la que conforman las personas originarias de Tlacuitapa, Jalisco, en México, y sus migrantes a ciudades en el norte de California y en Oklahoma en Estados Unidos. La primera vez que visitaron Tlacuitapa fue en enero de 2005, y varios equipos han regresado cada tres años desde entonces. Sin embargo, el responsable del programa, el profesor Wayne Cornelius, había investigado el fenómeno migratorio en Tlacuitapa a partir de 1976. Desde aquellos años no se ha dejado de indagar sobre las razones de la migración de los tlacuitapenses, sobre los efectos de las políticas migratorias en sus pobladores –migrantes y no-, y sobre el uso de las remesas. Se han estudiado también diversos asuntos sobre cómo los tlacuitapenses manejan sus medios de vida, educación, y salud mediante la construcción de la comunidad binacional (ver Cornelius y Lewis, 2007; Cornelius, FitzGerald y Borger, 2009 y FitzGerald, Alarcón y Muse-Orlinoff, 2011).

De esta forma, los temas de investigación de las decenas de estudiantes que se han formado en MMFRP, guiados por profesores de universidades en Estados Unidos y México, han tratado también sobre aspectos de transición familiar, de construcción de redes comunitarias, de participación en el mercado laboral, de aspiraciones educativas y transiciones culturales; además, han estudiado temas de salud como salud reproductiva, salud laboral, el acceso y la utilización de servicios de salud, y cambios de la alimentación.

En el trabajo de campo más reciente, llevado a cabo en enero de 2013, los datos recopilados tuvieron el propósito de facilitar el entendimiento de dos asuntos particulares en el momento histórico que se atravesaba. Además de las razones para emigrar frente a la crisis económica en Estados Unidos, agravada desde 2008, el primero tomó en cuenta la percepción de la recién aprobada Acción Diferida para los Llegados en la Infancia (DACA, por sus siglas en inglés) aprobada por el presidente Obama en junio de 2012. El segundo asunto de interés fue resultado de la acumulación de datos en las investigaciones previas sobre salud. De ello, se desarrollaron preguntas sobre el acceso a los servicios de salud, el manejo de enfermedades crónicas, la percepción sobre el VIH y el afrontamiento a los riesgos laborales. Estos temas son los que conforman el cuerpo de este libro. El segundo capítulo aborda el tema de las decisiones de migar y el conocimiento sobre DACA entre los talcuitapenses. A partir del tercer capítulo y hasta el último, los asuntos de salud son los que ocupan la mayor parte del libro.

Tlacuitapa es parte del municicpio de Unión de San Antonio en la región de Los Altos de Jalisco. Esta comunidad tiene una larga historia de migración a Estados Unidos que comenzó a principios del siglo XX. Los destinos más comunes de los tlacuitapenses han sido desde entonces Texas, California y Oklahoma. En esos lugares -y algunos otros como Illinois, Michigan, Nevada y Oregon - se han construido extensas redes sociales, se ha adquirido la residencia legal y la naturalización junto a una creciente segunda generación de migrantes (Cabrera-Hernández et al., 2011).

En los años recientes, el perfil de la migración en Tlacuitapa ha tenido algunas transformaciones. Gracias a las respuestas de los entrevistados en 2013, es posible conocer que el número de personas que emigran por primera vez ha disminuido, y que California ya no es la entidad principal de elección para quienes emigran por primera vez, ahora lo es Oklahoma. No obstante la reducción de nuevas migraciones, el cruce de frontera de forma ilegal sigue ocurriendo. El 86 por ciento de los entrevistados que fueron detenidos en su primer cruce, lo intentaron de nuevo pudiendo ingresar a Estados Unidos en su segundo o tercer intento (ver capítulo 2).

El asunto de la permanencia o el retorno entre los migrantes tlacuitapenses ha estado presente desde la primera visita del MMFRP. En aquel entonces López, Oliphant y Tejeda (2007) identificaron que el reforzamiento de la frontera, el mercado laboral y el uso de servicios sociales –tales como educación, servicios de salud, servicios asistenciales y compensación por desempleo- tenían impacto en la tendencia al asentamiento en Estados Unidos.

De forma semejante, durante el trabajo de campo del 2007, un equipo de cuatro estudiantes se preocupó por saber por qué los migrantes de Tlacuitapa deciden asentarse en Estados Unidos. Así, Jarvis et al. (2009) encontraron que la decisión de permanecer se construía como una consecuencia no intencionada de hacer la estancia más prolongada, ya fuera por el reforzamiento de la frontera o por el aumento de interacción con la sociedad estadounidense.

Dentro de las investigaciones del trabajo realizado en 2010, el asunto de la recesión económica ya estaba presente, por ello un número mayor de participantes del MMFRP se interesaron por entender el impacto de ello en la permanencia de migrantes. Puentes, Hong y Valencia (2011) encontraron que los talcuitapenses que vivían en ese entonces en Estados Unidos, no tenían planes de regresar a México aún frente a la crisis, en esos momentos preferían esperar a que esta se resolviera, que volver a la incertidumbre del empleo en su lugar de origen. Sin embargo, en la decisión de permanecer algunas prácticas necesitaban ser modificadas, esto es lo que hallaron por su lado Cabrera-Hernández et al (2011), cuando los entrevistados referían reducir la cantidad de envío en las remesas, tener un segundo trabajo, o autoemplearse.

En el capítulo 2, titulado "¿Asentarse o regresar?, qué importa más en las decisiones de los migrantes", los autores pretenden conocer por qué a pesar de la recesión económica en Estados Unidos y de los álgidos debates sobre una posible reforma migratoria, no hay menoscabo en la migración indocumentada. En particular, la pregunta gira alrededor de los factores –económicos, políticos y sociales- que determinan el proceso de toma de decisión para asentarse en Estados Unidos o para regresar a México, sobre todo a raíz de la recesión iniciada en 2008.

Los factores políticos tales como el reforzamiento de la frontera, una posible reforma migratoria y al aprovechamiento de la recién aprobaba DACA, no tuvieron un impacto importante en las decisiones sobre asentarse o regresar. Los factores tomados en cuenta de manera más significativa, fueron los económicos y sociales. Entre los motivos para asentarse surgieron una mayor percepción de bienestar, la amplitud del mercado laboral y la posibilidad de obtener mejores sueldos. Esto último representó en su forma contraria la razón más importante para regresar, es decir, determinó el retorno de aquellos en que la crisis provocó una disminución en su salario.

Cuatro temas sobre salud capturaron la atención de los participantes del MMFRP en 2013. El acceso a los servicios de salud, el manejo de la diabetes como padecimiento crónico, el riesgo de adquirir VIH y la salud laboral. Todos ellos, asuntos de interés global dado el aumento en los movimientos migratorios y la necesidad de construir redes de apoyo a la salud. La transición epidemiológica en México y Estados Unidos ha colocado a las enfermedades crónicas como principal causa de muerte, dejando atrás a las enfermedades infecciosas (WHO, 2011). Lo anterior requiere una mayor utilización de los servicios de salud, provocando en un contexto de migración como el de Tlacuitapa, mayor vulnerabilidad de los individuos frente a dos sistemas de salud disimiles, que no logran cubrir sus necesidades.

Adicionalmente, el tipo de empleos en los que insertan quienes emigran y el aumento de la participación en el mercado laboral de quienes permanecen en el lugar de origen, han hecho crecer el riesgo de sufrir enfermedades laborales e incapacidades temporales o permanentes. Con respecto a VIH, la migración aumenta el riesgo de transmisión del virus dada la inestabilidad económica, la separación de las familias, la falta de acceso a servicios de salud, y la cercanía a drogas inyectables y prostitución

(Ojeda et al., 2012; Brouwer et al., 2009). Cada uno de estos temas sanitarios, son centrales en las preguntas de investigación de este volumen.

En 2004, en MMFRP se investigó el uso de los servicios de salud como indicador de la integración de los migrantes a la sociedad estadounidense. López et al. (2007) encontraron que a medida que las familias tlacuitapenses se vuelven más establecidas en los Estados Unidos, son más propensas a utilizar cuidado de salud. También se dieron cuenta de que los migrantes cuya residencia primaria se mantiene en México son menos propensos a usar los servicios de salud en los Estados Unidos, y regresan con frecuencia a su lugar de origen en caso de que se sufran daños a su salud.

Bajo esta premisa, el capítulo 3 explora las barreras actuales de los tlacuitapenses residentes en Estados Unidos para el cuidado de su salud. Los migrantes entrevistados expresaron sentir temor al utilizar servicios de salud principalmente por el estatus migratorio irregular, por el costo de los servicios, y por la falta de comunicación entre usuarios y profesionales de salud. En este sentido, fueron los migrantes indocumentados quienes experimentaban mayormente, el temor por estatus migratorio. Las otras barreras identificadas fueron discriminación, idioma, y costos de los servicios. Una diferencia a destacar entre los migrantes residentes de California y de Oklahoma, es que los últimos tienen menor acceso a los servicios de salud, posiblemente por las medidas antiinmigrantes reforzadas en la última década en ese estado.

Considerar al temor como una barrera salió a la luz conforme se avanzaba en el trabajo de campo, dado que fue una de las expresiones más comunes que utilizaban los entrevistados para explicar por qué no acudían a clínicas u hospitales. De forma interesante, se encontraron antecedentes sobre esa barrera específica desde la visita a Tlacuitapa en 2007, donde el acceso a salud era limitado particularmente para los migrantes indocumentados por el temor a ser deportados y por la falta de información sobre el funcionamiento del sistema de salud. También se identificaron barreras como la discriminación y el idioma.

Como parte del acceso a servicios de salud, se habían estudiado en Tlacuitapa los padecimientos que creaban esa necesidad, y entre ellos apareció la diabetes en la investigación de 2007. En el trabajo de Oristian et al.

(2009) se muestra que desde el punto de vista de los profesionales de salud públicos y privados en el pueblo, las principales razones de consulta fueron las complicaciones de la diabetes. Asimismo, los tlacuitapenses migrantes y no migrantes, reportaron padecer algunas enfermedades; entre ellas, ocupó el cuarto lugar la diabetes. Una de las posibles explicaciones para ello en aquel momento fue el cambio de prácticas de salud en la comunidad binacional, especialmente los hábitos de nutrición y de forma particular en el grupo de migrantes, al enfrentarse a cambios socioculturales en los lugares de destino.

En relación a esto, el capítulo 4 nos muestra cómo puede caracterizarse la búsqueda de atención de los tlacuitapenses, pensando de forma concreta en las prácticas que beneficiarían a las personas con diabetes. La diabetes es una preocupación creciente de la salud pública, en México y en Estados Unidos. En este país la prevalencia se triplicó de 1990 a 2010 (CDC, 2011), y está aumentando su presencia en la población latina en comparación a otras poblaciones (CDC, 2012).

Es así que las preguntas que guían este capítulo titulado "Manejo de la enfermedad crónica: diabetes y la búsqueda de atención en una comunidad binacional de migrantes" son ¿cuál es la dinámica de interacción de los usuarios tlacuitapenses con los servicios de salud? y ¿cuáles son sus prácticas de nutrición y ejercicio? Para entender la dinámica de interacción, se observó lo relacionado a ciertas prácticas de prevención-realizar una prueba de detección de diabetes, recibir información sobre el padecimiento y visitar a un médico familiar-. Para conocer las prácticas de nutrición y ejercicio, se preguntó a los entrevistados por el tipo de alimentos que consumían diariamente y por la cantidad de ejercicio en el trabajo, labores del hogar o actividades de esparcimiento.

Como parte de los hallazgos, se encontró que los hombres tlacuitapenses en particular, parecen más aislados del sistema de salud en ambos países que las mujeres. Esto afecta considerablemente a los migrantes que viven de manera irregular en Estados Unidos. Sobre todo cuando resultó que la experiencia migratoria, el estatus legal y el acceso a educación tuvieron significativa importancia en la cantidad de información recibida sobre la diabetes. El tipo de alimentación no resultó óptima para prevenir la diabetes, sin embargo al estudiar las diferencias por género, se identificó a las mujeres como consumidoras de alimentos más favorables para conservar una buena salud. No obstante lo anterior, hay pocas prácticas preventivas y de control en la población de estudio.

Un tema que ha estado presente desde inicio del trabajo de MMFRP con esta comunidad es el de salud ocupacional; tratándose de una comunidad con añeja tradición migratoria, el tema del mercado laboral se ha estudiado desde el primer contacto con Tlacuitapa. Al cuestionarse sobre la inserción laboral en Estados Unidos, y al observar la transformación del lugar de origen con sus nuevos mercados de trabajo y las modificaciones en los roles de género, surgió también la pregunta: ¿qué efecto tienen en la salud los oficios más comunes y los nuevos tipos de trabajo? Si hace décadas atrás el trabajo más común en México y en Estados Unidos fue la agricultura, con el lapso del los años, la construcción y los servicios han tomado los primeros sitios. Lo anterior fue observado por miembros de MMFRP en Tlacuitapa y ciudades de destino en las visitas de 2004 y 2007.

Estos hallazgos junto a la ampliación del mercado laboral en el pueblo, con la instalación de una fábrica de zapatos en 2004, abrió mayores posibilidades de empleo para quienes no emigran y para las mujeres. Pero en ambos lados de la frontera, era necesario conocer los riegos a qué se enfrentan los trabajadores tlacuitapenses y la forma en que atienden los accidentes de trabajo. Se había conocido entonces, gracias al trabajo de Oristian et al (2009) que algunos migrantes Tlacuitapenses tuvieron que regresar a México para recibir tratamiento o esperar hasta que sus lesiones sanaran.

Recientemente, uno de los estudios de 2013 se enfocó a conocer en cuál país –México o los EE.UU. -- son tlacuitapenses más seguros en cuanto a su salud en el trabajo. A la fecha, la mayor parte de estudios sobre salud laboral se enfocan a trabajadores de la agricultura (ver Sakala, 1987; Schenker y McCurdy, 1990; Mobed et al., 1992; Stallones et al., 2009; McCauley et al., 2006). Sin embargo, en décadas recientes, el tipo de empleo ha cambiado entre los Tlacuitapenses, dejando por debajo el número de aquellos que se dedican a la agricultura.

A través de las páginas de capítulo 5 es posible conocer los riesgos del trabajo y los accidentes o incapacidades más comunes entre los tlacuitapenses y la forma en que se enfrentan a ellos en ambos países. Para profundizar en esta cuestión, el grupo de estudiantes que diseñó la pregunta, se enfocó a cuatro indicadores sobre salud laboral: la seguridad percibida en el lugar de trabajo, los abusos o accidentes experimentados, las agravios reportados, y la búsqueda de atención médica. Entre los resultados obtenidos, se reconoció que las lesiones en el trabajo son mayores para los tlacuitapenses en Estados Unidos que en México, particularmente los hombres, debido a sus ocupaciones entre las que predomina la construcción.

Por otro lado, para los trabajadores residentes en Tlacuitapa, las pocas opciones de empleo hacen que sean las mujeres las de mayor riesgo, dado que ellas conforman el mayor número de obreros en la localidad. Los abusos más comunes en ambos países son el robo de salario y el abuso verbal, sin embargo, el riesgo de sufrir este tipo de abusos aumenta después de haber migrado, debido a las barreras de idioma y al estatus migratorio. Las lesiones en el trabajo se reportan con mayor frecuencia en Estados Unidos, pero es frecuente que no se reporten a la autoridad correspondiente. En conclusión, se da a saber que entre los tlacuitapenses residiendo en ambos países, hay pobres condiciones de salud laboral.

Por último, el capítulo 6 retoma las investigaciones previas de MMFRP sobre salud sexual en Tlacuitapa, comenzadas en 2007 con un análisis de dinámica de género (Muse-Orlinoff et al., 2009), y seguidas por una discusión del uso del condón analizada en 2010 (Goldenberg, Kessler and Quesada, 2011). En este capítulo se analiza el riesgo de contagio de VIH y Enfermedades de Transmisión Sexual (ETS) construido socialmente entre los tlacuitapenses.

Como se mencionó antes, los migrantes mexicanos a Estados Unidos son particularmente vulnerables a la infección por VIH. En la actualidad, numerosos casos de VIH entre mujeres en áreas rurales en México se han relacionado con hombres migrantes infectados en Estados Unidos, que transmiten la infección a sus parejas a su regreso (Rangel et al. 2006). Por la larga tradición migratoria de Tlacuitapa y sus normas sexuales conservadoras, se investigaron las actitudes y prácticas del uso del condón como forma de prevención de VIH. En el análisis se tomaron en cuenta las conductas riesgosas y las relaciones sexuales en un contexto sociocultural, sin olvidar las estructuras institucionales que facilitan el riesgo de ETS. Entre esas estructuras se encuentran la vigilancia fronteriza cada vez más dura, que eleva el estatus social de los hombres migrantes que cruzan exitosamente la frontera, y de los cuales algunos se establecen en Estados Unidos.

Uno de los hallazgos de esta investigación fue la discrepancia entre las actitudes del uso del condón y de la practicas de la sexualidad, Aunque los entrevistados reconocieron la efectividad del condón en la prevención de VIH, reportaron un uso relativamente bajo del mismo. Argumentamos que tales disparidades entre actitudes y prácticas pueden deberse a las normas conservadoras en Tlacuitapa que desalientan el sexo pre-marital, y que fomentan el uso del rumor como forma de control social de la virginidad femenina. No obstante ello, los tlacuitapenses que viven en Estados Unidos, reconocieron el uso del condón como un medio socialmente aceptado de prevención de VIH y ETS.

METODOLOGÍA

El MMFRP tiene como objetivo explorar y documentar los cambios en la migración y el asentamiento, mediante el estudio de tres comunidades con historias de migración en México y sus comunidades satélite en los Estados Unidos. El trabajo de campo se lleva a cabo cada año por un equipo binacional de cerca de treinta estudiantes de pregrado y posgrado bilingües de ambos países. Los entrevistadores son capacitados por el programa para llevar a cabo las encuestas cuantitativas, observaciones etnográficas y entrevistas semi-estructuradas.

A pesar de que los matices de la investigación varían de año en año, hemos seguido investigando el impacto de las políticas de inmigración de Estados Unidos sobre los flujos migratorios y los patrones de asentamiento. Desde 2005, nuestro equipo ha estado documentando la eficacia y las consecuencias no deseadas de la estrategia de vigilancia de la frontera EE.UU. Estos estudios proporcionan la evidencia más reciente y directa de los patrones migratorios actuales. Tres sitios de estudio de MMFRP fueron seleccionados deliberadamente con el fin de explorar las hipótesis en una variedad de contextos socioeconómicos, culturales, y migratorios. Cada ciudad es relativamente pequeña, con 1,300 a 2,900 habitantes.

Durante el trabajo de campo en las comunidades de origen mexicano, los estudiantes tratan de entrevistar a todos los adultos de 18 a 65 años de edad en la localidad. Toda la población adulta de la comunidad se entrevista, de forma que se disminuyen los márgenes de error por muestra limitada. No se pretende que los datos resultantes sean estadísticamente representativos de toda la población mexicana, o de todos los migrantes mexicanos. Sin embargo, la variedad entre los sitios seleccionados son ampliamente representativos de las comunidades migratorias en México.

En las comunidades de migrantes en los Estados Unidos, se construyó una muestra con la técnica de la bola de nieve. Se hicieron entrevistas en las comunidades satélite en Estados Unidos durante los dos meses posteriores a la visita a México, esto último gracias a la información obtenida en el lugar de origen para tener contacto con amigos y familiares. Las encuestas estandarizadas para el estudio de 2013, se programaron en tabletas electrónicas. Las tabletas permitieron racionalizar y simplificar las fases de diseño, implementación y análisis, lo que permite a los estudiantes llevar a cabo entrevistas con mayor eficacia. Durante la fase de formación del programa, los estudiantes reciben entrenamiento en aspectos éticos de la investigación. Dada la gran sensibilidad de los temas de migración y salud, los entrevistadores respetaron estrictamente el derecho de la persona entrevistada a negarse a participar o a responder a preguntas específicas.

AGRADECIMIENTOS

Los habitantes de Tlacuitapa en ambos lados de la frontera han colaborado generosamente con la investigación de MMFRP. Estamos muy agradecidos con ellos por compartir sus historias personales, y nos sentimos honrados por su amabilidad a medida que aprendemos y crecemos en todo el proceso de investigación. Queremos agradecer a la Ford Foundation, al Center for American Progress, al Eleanor Roosevelt College, y a la Vicerrectoría para Equidad, Diversidad, e Inclusión de la Universidad de California en San Diego por su apoyo financiero para MMFRP, y a la Universidad de Guadalajara por apoyar la publicación de este libro.

Gathering of returned migrants from the United States during Tlacuitapa's annual fiestas. (Photo by Wayne Cornelius)

2   To Settle or to Return? What Matters Most in Migrants' Decisions

Hillary S. Kosnac, Yarazel Mejorado, Sarah M. Davidson, Moisés Marroquín And Celestino Nazario

> *My idea was to go back to Tlacuitapa. It was to go north for a little bit and then return. But it's been 35 years, and I still haven't returned, right? I still want to return.*—Pablo, a 50-year-old migrant settled in the United States

> *Immigration and the U.S.-Mexico relationship are linked. It's not just about coming and going. It's an exchange of people, society... everything.*—Juan, a 32-year-old migrant who spends his time divided between the United States and Mexico.

> *My roots are here. They gave me the opportunity to get papers, but I have never liked the life over there. Running, running... lots of running.*—Jorge, a 70-year-old migrant, describes why he chose to return to Mexico

Comprehensive immigration reform, blocked by partisan stalemates in 2006 and 2007, was once again on the Congressional agenda in 2013. Although various immigration reform bills have been proposed in the interim, the latest push for reform came as a bipartisan response to the prominent role played by Latino voters in the 2012 presidential election. Latinos played a critical role in the defeat of Republican presidential candidate Mitt Romney, who lost 70 percent of the Latino vote, largely as a result of his and the Republican Party's hard-line, anti-immigration rhetoric (Lopez and Taylor, 2012). In the newly elected Congress both parties quickly signaled that the time was right for revisiting immigration reform.

As in the 2006 and 2007 Congressional debates on immigration, the most contentious issue was creating a path to legalization for undocumented immigrants already living in the United States. The backdrop to this debate is the persistence of a very large stock of unauthorized immigrants, mostly from Mexico, living in the United States. According to Hoefer, Rytina and Baker's (2012) report for the Department of Homeland Security's Office of Immigration Statistics, the number of unauthorized immigrants residing in the United States remained at 10.8 million despite the Great Recession, increased spending on immigration enforcement, and a record-setting number of deportations during the Obama administration, averaging about 400,000 per year. Using its own methodology, the Pew Hispanic Center (2013) estimated that the stock of undocumented immigrants dropped by only 900,000 from its peak of 12 million in 2007 to 11.1 million in 2011.

Nevertheless, media reports claimed that the Great Recession had prompted a mass exodus of immigrants to Mexico (Suro and Zenteno, 2012). Moreover, tougher immigration enforcement at the border and in the U.S. interior had been expected to reduce the size of the undocumented population, both by discouraging new illegal entries and inducing large numbers of unauthorized immigrants to "self-deport," as Mitt Romney advocated during the 2012 campaign (Landsberg, 2012). The failure of both adverse labor market conditions and a hostile policy environment to make a significant dent in the U.S. stock of unauthorized immigrants is the puzzle we seek to unravel in this chapter.

This study explores the relative importance of economics, immigration policies, and social factors in the decisions that Tlacuitapenses make about migrating to the United States and settling there. Our research provides support for the well-established finding that economic considerations are predominant in the decision to migrate. Although a large body of research exists on this phase of the decision-making process, there has been much less attention on the factors influencing migrants' decisions to either settle in the United States or return to Mexico.

Our interviews with Tlacuitapenses on both sides of the border enable us to understand why, despite a severe economic recession and tougher immigration enforcement; some migrants have chosen to stay in the United States. For those who settle in the United States, economic conditions, closely followed by social considerations, are dominant in their decision-making. In addition to the economic benefits, Tlacuitapenses have remained in the United States because their children have been born there. We also examine the decision-making process of migrants who have chosen to return to Tlacuitapa and find economic factors, namely a decrease in wages, play the most influential role. The relative lack of importance that Tlacuitapenses attach to U.S. immigration laws and policies challenges the conventional wisdom that tougher border enforcement and interior immigration controls are an efficient way to deter unauthorized immigrants from entering and to induce them to go home if they have entered the United States.

LITERATURE REVIEW

It is surprising how many migrants have made the decision to stay put, considering that settlement in the United States is not usually their initial goal (McKeown, 1999). Bhatt and Roberts (2012), found that the original motivations of an individual migrant greatly influence the decision to settle or return. A substantial amount of research exists to support economic considerations as the primary motivation in the decision to migrate. If Bhatt and Roberts' finding holds, the decision to settle or return then should be influenced primarily by economic factors. This mode of explanation is consistent with widespread expectations that the economic recession would result in a large-scale return of immigrants to Mexico.

However, Rendall, Brownell, and Kups (2011) found that in past U.S. economic recessions (in the 1970s, 1980s, and 1990s), there actually has been a decline in return migration and an increase in settlement. Their study explains this counterintuitive phenomenon by utilizing the target-earner hypothesis, which holds that an immigrant's return to his/her country of origin is dependent on a planned level of earnings. It follows that during times of recession immigrants actually will stay longer, since labor market conditions require more time to achieve their desired amount of savings. In prior research among members of the Tlacuitapense community, Puentes,

Hong, and Valencia (2011) found evidence of significant U.S. settlement even during a recession, noting that 93 percent of Tlacuitapenses preferred to stay in the United States rather than return to Mexico.

In addition to economic conditions, Durand and Massey (2004) found that U.S. immigration policies play a role in the decision to settle in the United States or return to Mexico. Specifically, they found the increasing militarization of the southwestern border has encouraged permanent, settled immigration by drastically altering the circular pattern of Mexican immigration in which immigrants would come to the United States for set amounts of time and then return to Mexico. Reyes (2004) noted the militarization of the border has increased the cost and level of difficulty associated with border crossing, resulting in an increased risk of not being able to re-enter the United States without going deeply into debt and/or taking greater physical risks. Suro and Zenteno (2012) found a decline in return migration or an increase in U.S. settlement, over a period of time that coincides with heightened immigration enforcement measures. Indeed, it appears that since the enforcement measures have been enacted more immigrants are choosing to settle in the United States while fewer are choosing to return. This is the "caging effect" of border enforcement cited by Roger Waldinger and Nelson Lim as an unintended consequence of stronger enforcement (Waldinger and Lim, 2009).

A panel of immigration experts convened by the National Research Council in 2010-2011 also concluded: "Among unauthorized Mexicans who have made it into the United States, increased border and interior enforcement have a strong negative effect on the likelihood of their returning to Mexico. Unauthorized migrants who are working are reluctant to return to Mexico, even for a short visit, because they risk losing their foothold in the U.S. economy—a fear exacerbated by the recession. Moreover, they would have to pay heavily to be smuggled back into the United States." The panel noted that this "caging effect" accounts for "a significant portion of the growth in the stock of undocumented Mexicans" during the post-1993 period of stronger enforcement" (Redburn et al., eds. 2011: 36).

In addition to the militarization of the border, subnational immigration control policies can also influence a migrant's decision to settle in the United

States or return to Mexico. "Attrition through (interior) enforcement" is a strategy aimed at making life so miserable for undocumented immigrants that they self-deport. This approach has become a core tenet of conservative immigration policy prescriptions since 2006. In a previous study of Tlacuitapenses in the United States, García et al. (2011) noted that local immigration enforcement activities created a hostile living environment for some Tlacuitapenses, especially those living in Oklahoma City. Nevertheless, despite Tlacuitapenses' alienation from the community and its political leaders, there was no evidence to support an increased propensity to return to Mexico as a result of the state and local immigration policies.

Further research highlights the importance of social factors such as education, social networks, and perceptions of local crime in a migrant's decision to settle in the United States or return to Mexico. Among Tlacuitapenses living in the United States, García and Barreno (2007) found that more settlers than non-settlers believe the United States affords greater opportunities to children and perceive it as a better place for children to be raised. Similarly, Jarvis et al. (2009) noted that enrollment of Tlacuitapenses' children in U.S. schools is a significant predictor of settlement in the United States.

Reyes (2004) observed a connection between the growth of transnational social networks and the decision to settle in the United States. As social networks become more developed, with more members of the household and community participating in immigration, the networks become self-perpetuating and lead to increased rates of U.S. settlement. Similarly, Puentes, Hong, and Valencia (2011) observed the self-perpetuating nature of social networks in the Tlacuitapense community. With transnational familial networks spanning more than four generations, these long-standing connections help to explain why, despite negative economic and policy circumstances, more Tlacuitapenses choose to settle in the United States instead of returning to Mexico.

Accordingly, a lack of such connections in the United States strongly influences a decision to return to one's country of origin. García and Barreno (2007) found that if a strong network does not anchor an immigrant family in the United States, specific incidents in family life, such as a death in the family or a serious illness, can precipitate return migration. Their research also shows how certain safety concerns in the United States can encourage return to Mexico. For example, perceptions of danger and criminality are especially important to families with young children, for whom exposure to urban phenomena like gangs, drugs, and crime encourage decisions to return to Mexico. It is with these varied economic, policy, and social factors in mind that we turn to descriptions of Tlacuitapense settlers in the United States and those who have chosen to return to Mexico.

WHO HAS SETTLED IN THE UNITED STATES?

For the purposes of our research, we defined "settled" migrants as persons who were not born in the United States and have been living in the United States for at least three years. This definition yielded a total of 124 settled Tlacuitapenses. Of these settlers, 80.2 percent were documented at the time of our interviews, reflecting the long, multi-generational history of Tlacuitapense migration. Beginning in the 1920s Tlacuitapenses began coming to the United States, as a result of economic opportunities in the United States and violence in Mexico due to the conflict between the Catholic Church and the central government known as the Cristero Rebellion. Tlacuitapenses also participated in the Bracero Program, a contract laborer program for short-term agricultural workers that operated between 1942 and 1964. After the program was abolished, Tlacuitapenses continued to migrate to the United States illegally (Alarcón, FitzGerald, and Muse-Orlinoff, 2011). Many Tlacuitapenses were able to gain legal status and eventually U.S. citizenship through the Immigration Reform and Control Act of 1986 (IRCA). Through family reunification processes, these newly-documented migrants were able to petition for "green cards" for their spouses and families (Jarvis et al., 2009).

As a consequence of Tlacuitapenses' four generations of migration to the United States, they have been able to develop large, transnational social networks that encourage settlement by new migrants from the town. These social networks can be measured by looking at where a migrant's spouse, nuclear family, and extended family live. Having a U.S.-born child is also an indicator of social networks in the United States. Figure 2.1 reports the percentage of settled Tlacuitapense migrants who have a spouse living in the United States, more nuclear and extended family members living in the United States, and at least one U.S.-born child. As evidenced by figure 2.1, Tlacuitapense settlers have a higher percentage of family members living in the United States across each social network indicator.

Figure 2.1 Measures of U.S. Social Networks Among Settled Tlacuitapenses

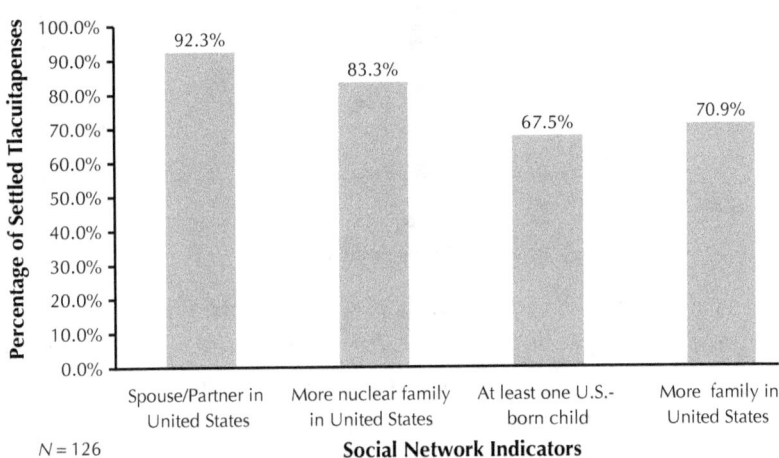

N = 126

However, a large social network of U.S.-based friends and family does not necessarily predict full integration into U.S. society. Although Tlacuitapense settlers tend to have large social networks in the United States, only 21.7 percent participate in any kind of political, social, or sports club there (See comparison to returned migrants' level of participation below). One possible impediment to such civic integration may be a lack of advanced English skills. A majority of settlers self-reported average English proficiency; 58.1 percent responded that they can speak only a little English and 52.0 percent can read only a little English.

Despite the Great Recession, settled Tlacuitapenses continue to rate the economy of the United States more favorably than the economy of Mexico (see figure 2.2).

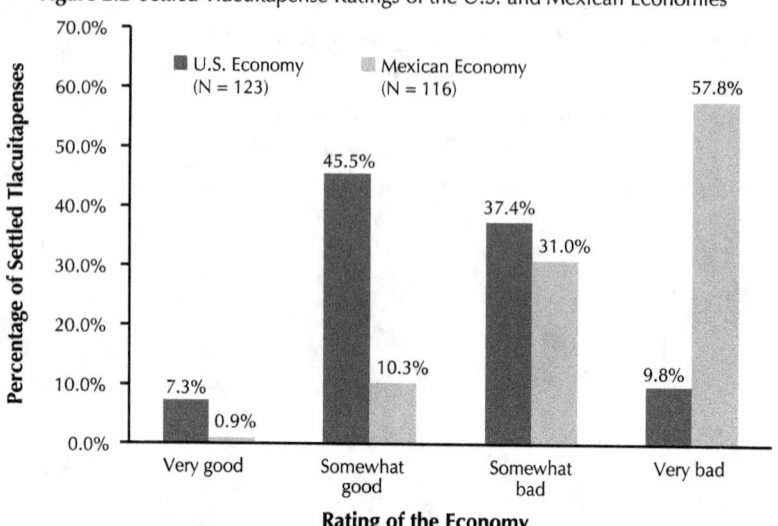

Figure 2.2 Settled Tlacuitapense Ratings of the U.S. and Mexican Economies

While a majority of settled Tlacuitapenses described the U.S. economy in positive terms, only 11.2 percent of settled Tlacuitapenses reported a positive view of the Mexican economy, despite relatively robust, national-level economic growth in Mexico in recent years. These statistics demonstrate that while U.S. economic conditions for Tlacuitapenses may not be ideal, settlers consistently view them more positively than those in Mexico. Lucía, a 60-year old settled migrant who resides in Union City, California, highlighted this comparison: "In the United States, the poorest person lives like someone who is rich here in Mexico." This manner of thinking may reflect the harsher economic realities of the Los Altos de Jalisco region where Tlacuitapa is located, compared with Mexico's national-level, macroeconomic situation. Tlacuitapenses' focus on the local opportunity structure in their home region could help to explain a decision to stay in the United States despite the economic recession there.

Favorable views of the U.S. economy could be a result of Tlacuitapenses' relative security in the labor market. According to the Bureau of Labor Statistics (2013a), the unemployment rate for Latinos in the United States was at 9.6 percent in February 2013. In comparison, of the 124 settled Tlacuitapenses whom we interviewed only 1.6 percent were openly unemployed at the time of our fieldwork. In addition to secure employment, Tlacuitapense settlers indicated receiving steady wages in the past five years. 91.6 percent of settlers have experienced the same or increasing wages since 2008.

Employment sector also plays an important role in settlement decisions. Riosmena (2004) found that agricultural workers had a higher propensity to return to Mexico than non-agricultural workers, due to the seasonal or temporary nature of the work in that sector. Figure 2.3[1] shows the most common economic activities for Tlacuitapense settlers. While about one-third worked in the construction industry and another 14.6 percent worked in manufacturing, just 2.4 percent of settled Tlacuitapenses worked in the agricultural sector (not shown in Figure 2.3).

Figure 2.3 Most Common Economic Activities for Settled Tlacuitapeses

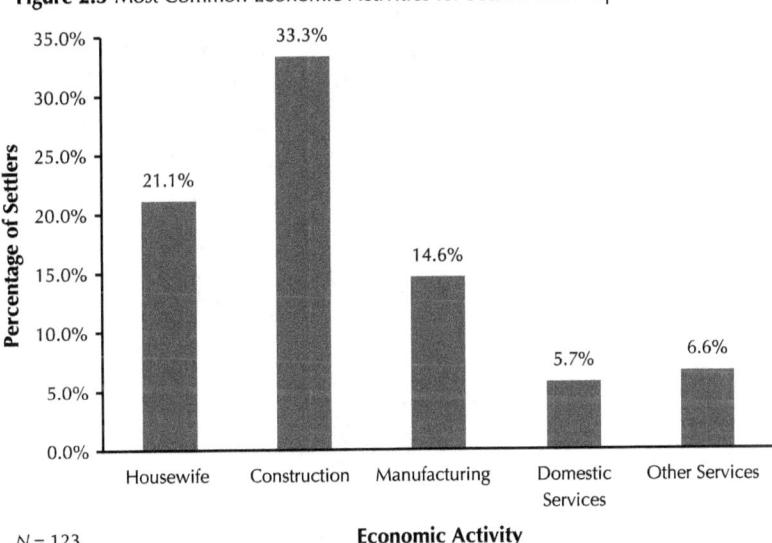

N = 123

Given the concentration of Tlacuitapenses in the construction industry, it is important to note that they typically work in large-scale, government-funded infrastructure projects, like bridge building, that have been relatively

---

1. The category of "Other Services" encompassed 0.8% in repair services (plumbing, carpentry, and mechanics), 2.5% in social services, and 3.3% in services related to food, recreation, and hospitality.

insulated from the recession, as opposed to residential construction. Previous studies have also found construction to be the most important source of jobs for Tlacuitapenses living in Oklahoma. This is attributable mainly to the fact that one of Tlacuitapa's former residents (who maintains a large home there) owns a successful Oklahoma City-based construction company that employs many Tlacuitapenses (Cabrera-Hernández, et al., 2011). In addition to low levels of unemployment, this concentration in more stable, non-seasonal jobs suggests Tlacuitapenses may be shielded from some labor-market factors that traditionally encourage return.

WHO HAS RETURNED TO MEXICO?

We define a "returned" migrant as a person who lived in the United States at any time between 2008 and 2012 and who currently lives in Mexico. This definition encompasses 38 interviewees. Of the returned migrants in our sample, 79 percent were male and 70.3 percent were undocumented. Among returnees, the last place of U.S. residence before returning to Mexico varied (see figure 2.4). The most commonly cited last place of U.S. residence was Oklahoma (35.1 percent) followed by the Chicago area and the Los Angeles area.

Figure 2.4 Returned Migrants' Last Location of U.S. Residence

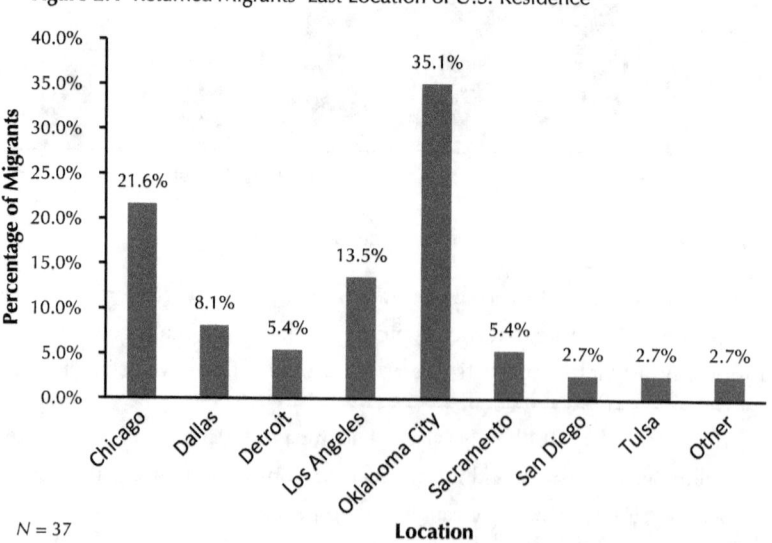

N = 37

Since the 1990s, Oklahoma City has attracted the largest number of Tlacuitapense migrants to the United States, so it follows that there has been a higher rate of return from Oklahoma (20.4 percent) as compared from California (9.2 percent) since 2008.

While 78.2 percent of settled Tlacuitapenses are married, only 60.5 percent of returnees are married. While in both groups we find high marriage rates, there is a marked contrast between them in terms of the size of their social networks in the United States. As evidenced in figure 2.5, across all indicators of U.S-social networks, Tlacuitapense returners have weaker social networks as compared to Tlacuitapense settlers.

Figure 2.5 Comparison of U.S-based Social Networks Between Returned and Settled Tlacuitapenses

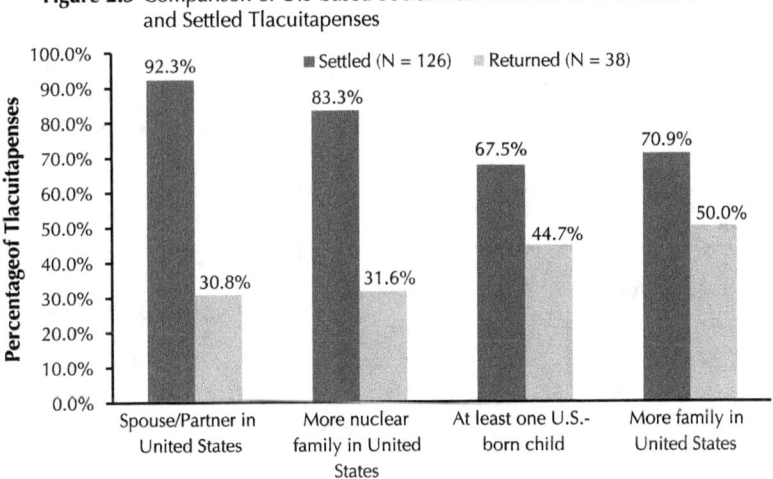

This difference suggests that a lack of social ties to the United States and a desire for family reunification could play a role in the decision to return to Mexico. Nevertheless, it is important to note that 34.2 percent of these migrants have children who still live in the United States. This finding may be surprising giving the stated cornerstone of U.S. immigration policy is family reunification.

Returned Tlacuitapenses also reported a lack of civic participation within their U.S. host community. None of the returned migrants whom we interviewed had participated in a U.S. social, political, or sports club. As with settled migrants, limited English proficiency could help to explain this lack of social participation. Nine out of ten returnees reported that they read little to no English, and 81.9 percent speak little to no English. But unauthorized status also could explain this hesitancy to participate. Carlos, a returned migrant in his thirties, described his experience in Oklahoma City: "I almost never left [my house]. If I had papers, I would have gone wherever I wanted. But, it's difficult for people there who don't have papers. It's very scary." Similar sentiment was felt by Marta, another returned migrant in her twenties, as she explained how she was afraid to drive in Oklahoma City due to her unauthorized status: "It was like I felt confined without the freedom to do anything. I felt useless."

To identify the specific sources of feelings about life in the shadows, we asked returned Tlacuitapenses what an undocumented migrant living in the city where the interviewee had lived in the United States worried about most. Respondents were asked to choose the three types of activities or occurrences that generated the most worry from the following options (see figure 2.6).

Figure 2.6 Worrisome Aspects of Living in the United States for Undocumented Migrants

As shown in figure 2.7, workplace raids were cited as the foremost concern by 52.8 percent of returned migrants. The second most commonly cited concern was driving a car, followed by concerns about going to a hospital.

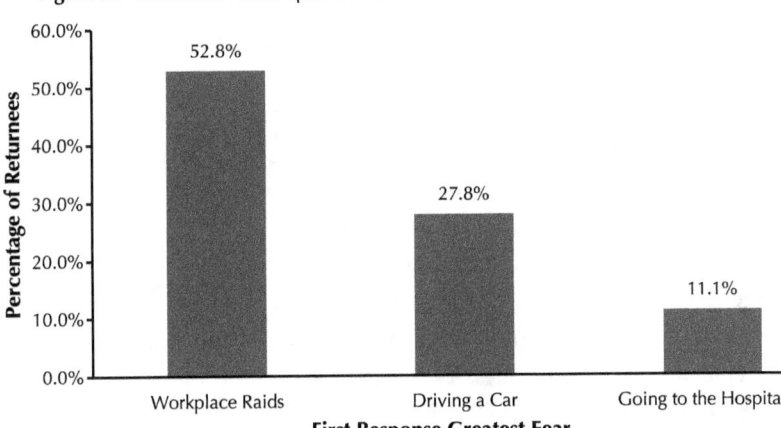

Figure 2.7 Returned Tlacuitapenses' Greatest Fears in the United States

Analyzing the responses to this question by last place of United States residence yields a more nuanced picture of the location-specific hardships encountered by Tlacuitapenses without papers. For example, among those who returned from Oklahoma, only the following three concerns were cited as the most worrisome aspect of migrant life in the United States: workplace raids (58.3 percent), driving a car (33.3 percent), and going to the hospital (8.3 percent). Responses of returned migrants from other U.S. locations were considerably more varied though workplace raids were the top-ranked concern by all respondents regardless of location. This suggests that, in Oklahoma, immigration enforcement efforts are more focused on certain aspects of a migrant's life (i.e., employment and driving) than in other U.S. destinations. Indeed, García et al. (2011) found that a series of restrictive state immigration laws in Oklahoma (especially HB 1804, which restricts undocumented migrants' access to a variety of services) increased the risk of deportation for migrants engaging in such activities as driving without a license.

In addition to fears about immigration enforcement, return migration can be precipitated by adverse economic conditions, such as lack of jobs or decreased wages. As noted above, previous studies have found the seasonal nature of agricultural work to be a strong predictor of return (Riosmena, 2004; Marcelli and Cornelius 2001). We did find an increase in the proportion of returnees working in agriculture as compared to settlers (13.1 percent and 2.4 percent, respectively). However, like settlers, a plurality of returned Tlacuitapenses (26.3 percent) had been working in construction in the United States.

Despite settled Tlacuitapenses being relatively insulated from the effects of the economic recession, returned Tlacuitapenses reported a different experience. Four out of five returned migrants reported a decrease in their wages in the United States before their return to Mexico. The average amount of decrease in overall income since 2008 was quite large—approximately $428 (U.S.) a week. This large wage decline could be indicative of a more serious trend, namely potential job loss, for returned Tlacuitapenses. Nevertheless, as Figure 2.8 demonstrates, returnees' perceptions of the U.S. economy largely paralleled those of Tlacuitapenses settled in the United States.

Figure 2.8 Settled and Returned Tlacuitapenses' Ratings of the U.S. Economy

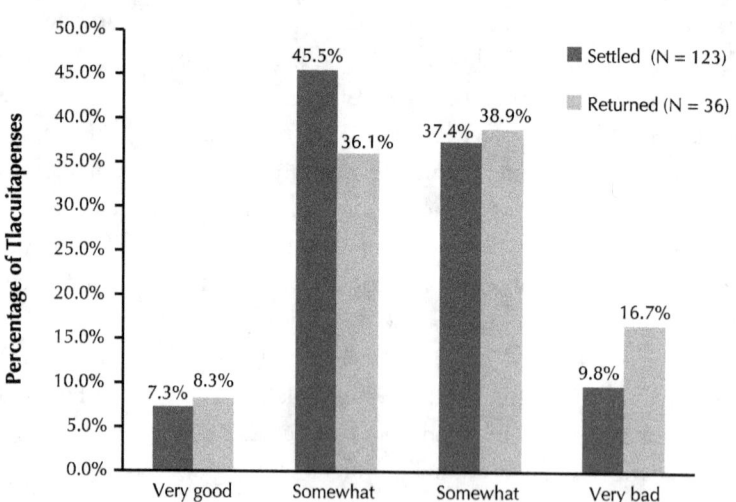

While around half of settlers and returnees held positive views of the U.S. economy, an overwhelming majority of both groups stated negative views of the Mexican economy, as shown in figure 2.9.

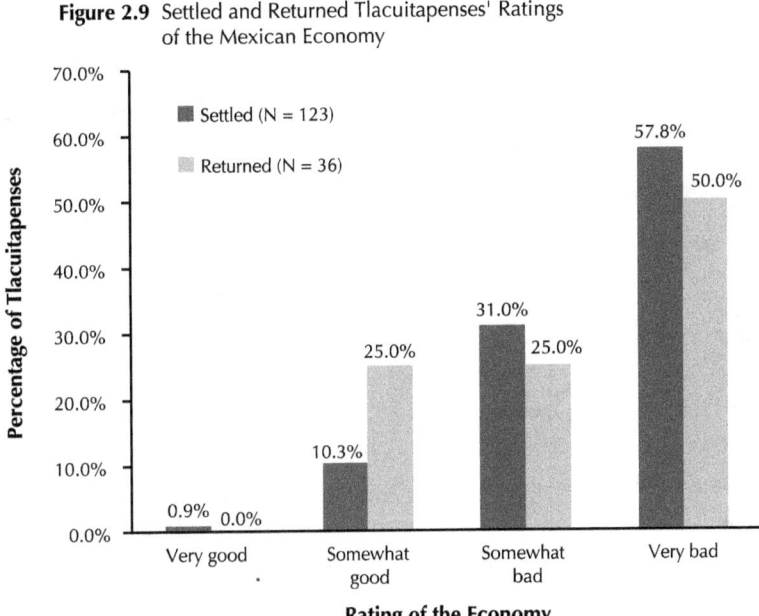

Figure 2.9 Settled and Returned Tlacuitapenses' Ratings of the Mexican Economy

It seems that the Tlacuitapenses' economic perceptions of the U.S. and Mexican economies do not significantly differ between those who have decided to settle or those who chose to return. The role of economic factors—not just perceptions—in Tlacuitapense decision-making will be discussed in further depth in the multivariate analysis that follows.

STAYING HOME "FOR GOOD"

An interesting subgroup of returned migrants are those who do not have plans to return to the United States. We define this subgroup as persons who have lived in the United States at any time between 2008 and 2012, currently live in Mexico, and have no plans to return to the United States in the year 2013. Twelve of our interviewees fit these criteria, all of whom are undocumented. Among this subgroup, the largest number of returned migrants is returning from Oklahoma (see figure 2.10).

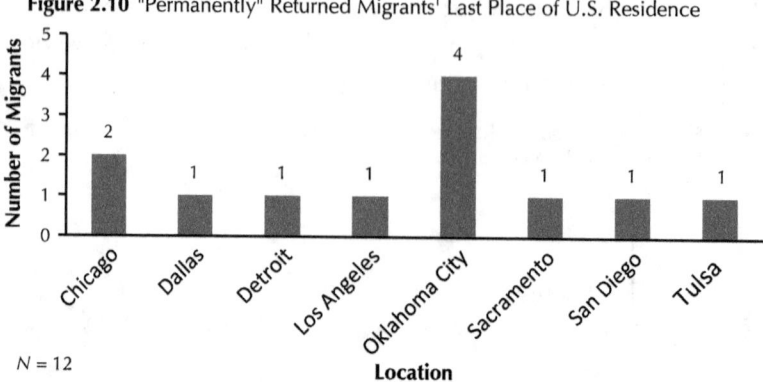

Figure 2.10 "Permanently" Returned Migrants' Last Place of U.S. Residence

N = 12

These findings perfectly mirror those of the broader returned migrant category in which Oklahoma and Chicago were the most commonly cited last cities of residence before returning.

Much like other returners, the majority of "permanent stay-at-home" returnees are male and married. Both categories of returners are also similar in that the strength of their U.S.-based social networks is quite weak as compared to settlers. Figure 2.11 compares the social network indicators among the three groups of migrants: settlers, returnees, and "permanent" returnees.

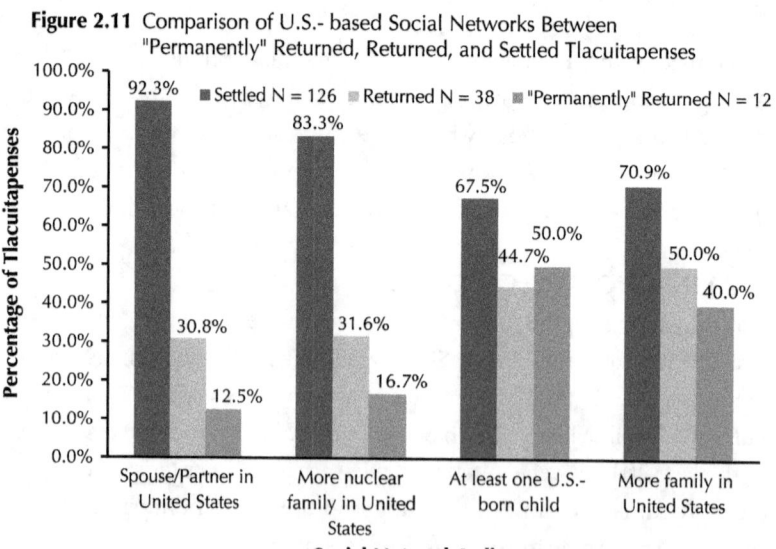

Figure 2.11 Comparison of U.S.- based Social Networks Between "Permanently" Returned, Returned, and Settled Tlacuitapenses

The most notable differences between settlers and those returnees who have no plans to return to the United States in 2013 are the location of their spouses and consequently their nuclear family. While over 90 percent of settlers indicated their spouse lives in the United States, the same proportion of "permanent" returnees reported their partner lives in Mexico. It is not surprising that almost half of the permanent returnees cited the desire for family reunification as the most important reason for going back to Mexico. Considering that members of this subgroup have no plans to return to the United States, this suggests the importance of family ties not only in promoting returns to Mexico but also in deterring future migration.

As among the broader category of returned migrants, having only a tenuous connection with the U.S. labor market seems to have influenced Tlacuitapenses who do not plan to go north again. Slightly more migrants in this subgroup had been working in agriculture (16.7 percent) as compared to 13.5 percent of all returners. Also, most had experienced a decline in wages during the years preceding their return to Mexico. Nine out of ten returned migrants indicated a decrease in wages since 2008. On average, among these "permanent" returnees there was approximately a $466 (U.S.) decrease in weekly income since 2008. Again, this sharp decline in wages could indicate unemployment before return. Among those returnees who have no plans to go back to the United States, one-third described the U.S. economy as "very bad," compared with 16.7 percent of those who do plan to migrate again. This difference suggests that perceptions of economic conditions in the United States are a strong determinant of decisions to migrate in the future.

Additionally, it is important to note that certain legal or policy factors can deter a Tlacuitapense's return to the United States, at least in the short term. The Illegal Immigration Reform and Immigrant Responsibility Act (IIRIRA) of 1996 instituted bans on re-entering the United States for migrants who had previously resided there without authorization for more than one year and were deported. Ten years was the most commonly imposed ban among the Tlacuitapenses whom we interviewed. These bans could help to explain the aforementioned 34.2 percent of returned migrants who have children that continue to live in the United States.

Tlacuitapenses who have been banned from re-entry cite the psychological impact of prolonged family separation as the most serious consequence. Mercedes, a 30-year old Tlacuitapense married to a U.S. citizen, explained: "[Living separated from my family] is the most difficult thing that has happened to me." She described how her family has faced economic problems as a result of paying for houses in two countries and how both of her young children have suffered psychologically as a result of the family separation. Marta, a mother of two U.S.-born children who also received a ten-year re-entry ban, echoed the psychological burdens of family separation: "My husband was diagnosed with depression because of [being separated]. The psychologist told him that it was because it was too little time here and too little time there....We are struggling a lot because of that."

A MULTIVARIATE ANALYSIS OF THE DECISION TO SETTLE OR RETURN
Modeling the Decision to Settle

To determine the relative importance of economic, public policy, and social factors in Tlacuitapenses' decisions to settle in the United States, we conducted a multiple regression analysis. The dependent variable, "settlement," is operationalized as having been born in Mexico, currently living in the United States, and having resided there for at least three years at the time of our interviews. The independent variables used in the model represent the economic, policy, and social factors that have been determined in previous research to be key predictors of settlement. As reported in table 2.1, we find that a Tlacuitapense migrant is significantly more likely to settle in the United States if he/she possesses legal status, has greater amounts of wealth, and has at least one U.S.-born child. Additionally, a Tlacuitapense is less likely to settle if he/she works in the agricultural sector in the United States or has experienced a decline in income since 2008.

Table 2.1 Factors in a Tlacuitapense's Decision to Settle in the United States

	Model 1	Model 2	Model 3
Age	-0.005*	-0.008***	-0.006*
Male	-0.112*	0.000	0.105
Wealth	0.246***	0.165***	0.207***
Has papers	0.410***	0.401***	0.278***
Has more family in the United States		0.092	0.136
Has a U.S.-born child		0.204**	0.198**
Works in agriculture			-0.251**
Has experienced a wage decline			-0.190*
Optimistic about a legalization program			-0.018
Has been detained			0.010
Constant	0.518***	0.448***	0.420**
N	242	171	103
R^2	0.438	0.493	0.650

This analysis suggests that a combination of economic and social variables is most influential in Tlacuitapenses' decisions to settle, a finding consistent with our qualitative interviews with settled Tlacuitapenses in the United States. When asked about the most important reason he continues to stay in the United States, Pablo, a settled migrant in Fontana, California, explained: "The number one [reason] for me, and I think for everyone else too, is the way of living here—the economy." However, earlier in the conversation, Pablo did acknowledge the secondary importance of social factors like having U.S. born children in the decision to settle: "I established myself and started a family; so [other] things start happening. Your children are studying [in school]. Your children are there." The secondary importance placed on social factors evidenced in our qualitative interviews is also consistent with our regression analysis.

Two caveats are in order. First, while we found wealth to be a significant predictor of settlement, we must consider the issue of directionality. It could be that migrants are deciding to settle not because they are wealthier but rather they are wealthier because they have decided to settle. Our qualitative evidence supports the latter explanation, in that many migrants left Tlacuitapa during their late teens or early twenties and have accumulated their wealth as a result of their decision to settle in the United States. Second, we did not include what may seem like an obvious variable in our model, i.e., having a spouse who lives in the United States, due to a lack of variance in our sample. Over 90 percent of settled migrants have a U.S.-based spouse. As a consequence, although we found only one social factor to be a statistically significant predictor of settlement, there are other social aspects of a migrant's life that are likely to be important in shaping settlement decisions.

In terms of policy effects, we asked respondents if they believed there would be a legalization program, or in other words, a program for unauthorized individuals living in the United States to adjust to authorized status, within the next four years. We found that expectations of a future legalization program are not a statistically significant predictor of the decision to settle. This finding might seem surprising, given the heated political and public rhetoric surrounding a path to citizenship for unauthorized migrants. In addition to a feared influx of new undocumented migrants, concerns over rewarding "bad behavior" and increasing the propensity of undocumented migrants already in the United States to settle have figured prominently in this debate. But our findings suggest that a legalization program would not encourage many more migrants to stay in the United States in hopes of gaining legal status. At the same time, caution should be exercised in generalizing this finding, since the absence of a relationship could reflect the heavy representation of permanent legal-resident migrants in our sample—individuals who would have no need for a new legalization program.

Modeling the Decision to Return

We estimated two separate regression models to analyze the relative importance of economic, policy, and social factors on the decision to return to Mexico. In the first model, the sample included any interviewee with U.S. migration experience who has ever returned to Mexico. In the second model, we included only those migrants who had returned between 2008 and 2012, coinciding with the Great Recession years. We then compare the results of these two models to gauge whether the recession and increased interior enforcement efforts affected the return decision process. Table 2.2 summarizes the results for our first model, including all Tlacuitapenses interviewed in Mexico who had ever returned from the United States. We find that a migrant is significantly more likely to return if he/she has lower wealth, does not have legal status in the United States, and does not have a U.S.-born child. However, when we focus on Tlacuitapenses who have returned to Mexico within the past five years in our second model, we find very different results. As shown in table 2.3, the only statistically significant predictor of return is a decline in wages. The previously significant predictors of return among the "ever returned migrant" category are no longer significant.

Table 2.2 Factors in a Tlacuitapense's Decision to Return to Mexico

	Model 1	Model 2	Model 3
Age	-0.051***	0.059***	0.075*
Male	0.545	0.015	-0.680
Wealth	-1.322***	-0.885**	-1.161*
Has papers	-1.973***	-1.662***	-1.985**
Has more family in the United States		-0.392	-0.052
Has a U.S.-born child		-1.116**	-1.980**
Last U.S. job in agriculture			-0.362
Experienced a wage decline in U.S.			1.101
Optimistic about a legalization program			-0.212
Has been detained			-0.776
Constant	-1.912**	-1.343	-1.163
N	243	172	103
R^2	0.314	0.326	0.454

Table 2.3 Factors in a Tlacuitapense's Decision to Return
to Mexico Since 2008

	Model 1	Model 2	Model 3
Age	-0.015	-0.017	0.014
Male	0.918*	0.844	0.549
Wealth	-0.280	-0.011	0.828
Has papers	-0.760	-1.190*	-2.236
Has more family in the United States		0.332	0.810
Has a U.S.-born child		0.139	0.055
Last U.S. job in agriculture			0.164
Experienced a wage decline in U.S.			4.684***
Optimistic about a legalization program			-0.021
Has been detained			-0.967
Constant	-1.377	-1.253	-4.531*
N	243	172	103
R^2	0.069	0.071	0.523

While a combination of economic, policy, and social factors helps to
explain Tlacuitapense migrants' decision to "ever return", the "recent
return" regression analysis clearly suggests economic factors have played
the most influential role in Tlacuitapenses' decisions to return during the
period since 2008. In order to determine if recession-related declines in
wage income increased returns among Tlacuitapenses, we compared rates
of return before and after 2008. Between 2008 and 2012 we estimate a 23.5
percent return rate, compared with a 15 percent rate of return between
2003 and 2008. Thus, the return rate for 2008-2012 is 44 percent higher
than in the previous five years.

This finding offers strong support for the notion that the Great Recession
did, in fact, encourage return migration among some Tlacuitapenses.
However, we must note that such returns may not be permanent. Among

our returned migrants, almost 70 percent had plans to go back to the United States in 2013. It is likely that as their job prospects in the United States improve, many of these returnees will go north again, as predicted by various analysts (see, for example, Suro and Zenteno 2012; Redburn, et al. 2011: 34-36).

In our post-2008 return regression social variables were not statistically significant, but many Tlacuitapenses continue to point to these factors as the key reason for their return to Mexico. In fact, among Tlacuitapenses who have returned to Mexico in the last five years, 37.1 percent reported a desire to reunite with family members as the most important consideration in their return. It is possible there is correlation between economic and social factors in that as stress mounts from economic concerns (e.g., lost wage income), a migrant may begin to yearn for his/her social network in Mexico, which then contributes to the decision to return. But this finding is also consistent with the perceptions of Tlacuitapenses who have ever returned to Mexico after living in the United States. Among this larger group of interviewees, almost half (45.3%) considered family reunification to be paramount in their decision to go home.

Compared to economic and social variables, policy factors related to interior enforcement do not seem to influence Tlacuitapenses' decisions to return. As a proxy for interior enforcement, we used the experience of being detained in the United States. This variable was not a significant predictor of return in either the "ever returned" or "recently returned" regression model. Although not statistically significant in explaining return migration, we did find that stepped-up interior immigration enforcement had affected an increased portion of the transnational Tlacuitapense community.

The percentage of Tlacuitapenses who reported that a family member had been deported in the past three years was much higher in our 2013 survey than in our 2010 study. More than one out of ten (12.6 percent) of all Tlacuitapenses interviewed in 2013 had experienced the deportation of at least one family member, an almost 50 percent increase from the rate reported in 2010 (8.6 percent). This finding reflects the record number of deportations under the Obama administration: approximately 400,000 per year, more than double the number of annual deportations in the first term of George W. Bush's presidency. Nevertheless, deportation affects a relatively low percentage of Tlacuitapenses, which explains the lack of significance in our regression models.

DEFERRED ACTION AND TLACUITAPENSE DECISION-MAKING

In the summer of 2012 a new policy initiative was implemented in the United States aimed at providing temporary conditional residency for undocumented individuals who came to the United States as children. More specifically, beginning in June 2012, Deferred Action for Childhood Arrivals (DACA) allows immigration enforcement officials to "defer removal of an undocumented person from the United States as an act of 'prosecutorial discretion'" (U.S. Citizenship and Immigration Services, 2013a). In order to qualify for deferment of deportation, applicants must meet strict age, education, and continuous U.S. residence requirements. Qualified applicants are eligible to receive authorization to work in the United States for the duration of their deferred status. There has been widespread speculation this initiative or any other legalization program would encourage an influx of new undocumented migrants or promote settlement in the United States by those already here. But we found DACA to be of little to no importance in Tlacuitapense migrants' decision-making.

Among our interviewees, the number who had even heard of the DACA program was very low. Only one out of five Tlacuitapenses (19.4 percent) reported some knowledge of DACA. Interestingly, as shown in figure 2.12, female Tlacuitapenses were much more knowledgeable with regard to DACA than males.

Figure 2.12 Knowledge of DACA by Gender

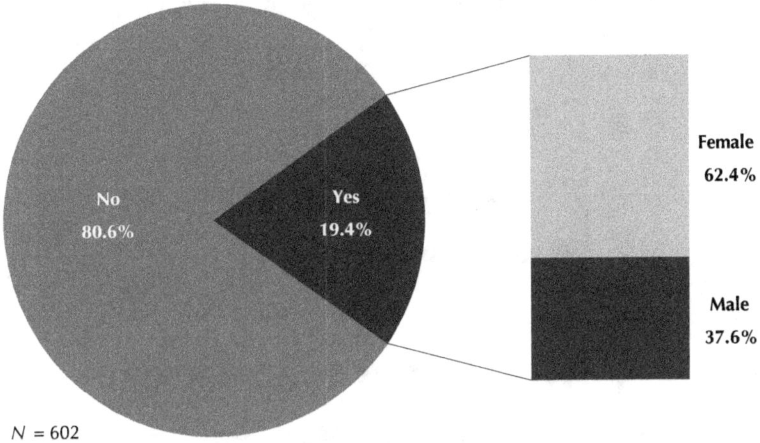

It is important to highlight that the familiarity of the initiative among Tlacuitapenses was largely nominal. Of those who knew of the program's existence slightly more than half (56.3 percent) knew one or more of the eligibility requirements for the initiative. When asked to list the requirements for Deferred Action, many respondents instead listed the requirements for the long-proposed Development, Relief, and Education for Alien Minors (DREAM) Act, which would provide a conditional permanent resident status for certain unauthorized individuals who came to the United States before the age of 15, have lived continuously there for five years, have graduated from high school, and are of good moral character. Conditional legal resident status could eventually lead to eligibility for U.S. citizenship. The confusion between DACA and DREAM Act illustrates the fragmented and incomplete dissemination of information regarding U.S. immigration policy developments within the Tlacuitapense community.

In order to further understand the dissemination of DACA-related information, we compared rates of knowledge on both sides of the border and between satellite communities of Tlacuitapenses within the United States. As shown in figure 2.13, we found that Tlacuitapenses living in the United States had greater knowledge of DACA than those in Mexico.

There were also significant differences in knowledge based on place of residence within the United States. A larger proportion of respondents living in Oklahoma City indicated knowledge of DACA compared to those living in the San Francisco Bay's Union City.

Figure 2.13 Knowledge of DACA by Location

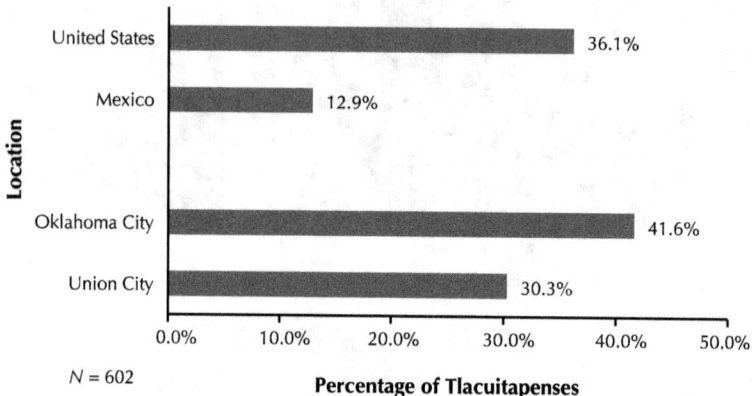

$N = 602$

A policy development like DACA only directly benefits those who are living in the United States without documentation, so it follows that interviewees in Oklahoma City, who were more likely to be undocumented, are more knowledgeable about DACA. However, we did not find a large difference in rates of knowledge between the documented (35.6 percent) and undocumented members of the U.S.-based Tlacuitapense population (39.3 percent). This finding suggests that the higher percentage of individuals with knowledge about DACA in Oklahoma City could be a result of greater outreach efforts concerning DACA in Oklahoma City compared with Union City.

In looking more specifically at these two regions, a few salient details emerge that could help to explain the differential rates of knowledge between Tlacuitapenses in Union City and Oklahoma City. First, while California has a greater absolute number of immigrants (350,000) who are currently eligible for DACA, Oklahoma has a greater eligibility density. Of Oklahoma migrants, it is estimated that between 4.8 and 9.6 percent are DACA-eligible compared to 3.4 percent of California's foreign-born population (Batalova and Mittlelstadt, 2012; Migration Policy Institute,

2013). State-level data for DACA applications suggests that in California 40.4 percent of those eligible have applied, compared to estimates between 20.5 and 41 percent in Oklahoma (U.S. Citizenship and Immigration Services, 2013b). Looking at data obtained from a Freedom of Information Act (FOIA) request on DACA applicants by zip code for the first 150,000 applicants, we found that in Oklahoma City, there had been 267 applicants. In Union City, there had been 45. This could potentially be one measure of the work organizations are doing on the ground in each of these locations.

Another way we could see if increased knowledge of DACA among Oklahoma-based Tlacuitapenses is a result of organizational efforts would be to look at the number of migrant-serving organizations in both locations. To determine the number of these organizations, we used GuideStar,[2] a group that collects information on each non-profit registered with the Internal Revenue Service (IRS). A search of GuideStar generates a listing of one migrant-serving organization in Union City and four in Oklahoma City. While utilizing GuideStar does not tell us specifically about organizations that provide DACA-related services, Own the Dream,[3] a website developed by United We Dream and other prominent migrant-serving legal organizations to aid DACA applicants, provides lists of legal resources for each state and county. According to Own the Dream, in Oklahoma there are five organizations listed that help individuals with DACA-applications, two of which are located in Oklahoma City. Comparatively, in California, there are 83 organizations that help with DACA. However, Own the Dream does not list any organization that provides DACA assistance in Union City. While there are organizations in the greater Bay Area, they are located about a half hour to forty-five minutes away from Union City. This suggests that distance could serve as a potential barrier for any outreach efforts these organizations attempt, which could help to explain the lower rates of knowledge among Union City-based Tlacuitapenses.

In order to determine the impact of DACA on Tlacuitapense's settlement decisions, we estimated the current number of DACA-eligible migrants in

2. http://www.guidestar.org/AdvancedSearch.aspx
3. http://www.weownthedream.org/legalhelp/

our survey population. Respondents' birth date, current place of residence, education, documentation status, age on most recent trip to the United States, and number of trips out of the United States were all included in the estimation procedure. We were unable to include one of DACA's eligibility requirements—a lack of previous criminal convictions—because no questions were asked about criminal record. Based on the other DACA eligibility requirements we determined that 8.2 percent of our U.S.-based interviewees could possibly qualify for the program. However, when asked if they knew anyone (including themselves) who could apply for DACA, not a single respondent answered affirmatively. Furthermore, of those eligible individuals, only one in four had even heard of the initiative. Given their lack of knowledge regarding eligibility for the program, we can conclude that DACA is not playing a role in Tlacuitapenses' decisions to settle in the United States.

RECENT MIGRATION TO THE UNITED STATES

While markedly reducing new migration to the United States, the Great Recession of 2008-2012 did not completely end Tlacuitapa's long history of northbound movement. During the 2008-2012 period, 39 of our interviewees made a trip to the United States, of whom 15 were undocumented. For purposes of our study, a trip was defined as lasting longer than a month, with the intent to live or work in the United States. The number of new migrations represents a decrease from the 55 migrants (35 of whom were undocumented) making their most recent trip to the United States in the previous five years (2002-2007). Thus, in the pre-recession period undocumented migrants made up 63.6 percent of the total Tlacuitapense migration flow to the United States, after 2008 they only accounted for only 38.5 percent (see figures 2.14 and 2.15).

Figure 2.14   Composition of Tlacuitapense Migration Flows, 2002-2007

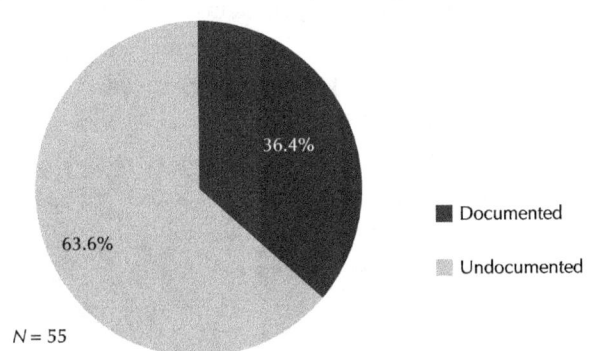

Figure 2.15   Composition of Tlacuitapense Migration Flows, 2008-2012

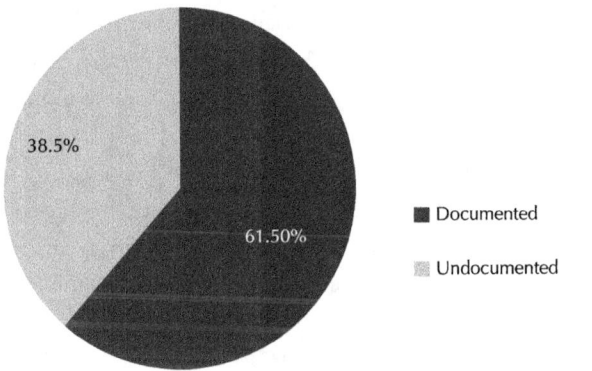

This sharp decrease in undocumented migration could be the result of depressed U.S. labor market conditions (Suro and Zenteno, 2012; Redburn, Reuter, and Majmundar 2011: 34). It could also reflect tougher U.S. border enforcement policies, which would only affect undocumented Tlacuitapenses. Carlos, a returnee interviewed in Tlacuitapa who had made two successful border crossings in previous periods, explained that he had no plans to go to the United States in 2013 because of these policies, which have increased difficulty in crossing: "For right now, no [I'm not thinking about returning to the United States].... It's really difficult right now. There's a lot of security. I've tried to go three times, and three times I returned [without entering]." Thus a perceived lower probability of successful entry may be discouraging some Tlacuitapenses from trying their luck at the border, at least in combination with higher people-smugglers' fees (see below) and uncertain job prospects in the United States.

Of those who made the journey north since 2008, virtually all of our undocumented interviewees—14 out of 15—hired a coyote, or people-smuggler, to assist them in crossing the border. This finding is consistent with previous research on coyote usage among Tlacuitapenses. Since at least 2000, coyotes have been seen as a necessity for Tlacuitapenses lacking papers (Sisco and Hicken, 2009). Coyotes are not only in higher demand in recent years but they are also demanding higher fees. We found that from 2000-2007 the average coyote fee paid by Tlacuitapenses was $2,100 (U.S.), which is in line with previous research among Tlacuitapense migrants (Hicken, Fishbein, and Lisle, 2011). In comparison, we found that Tlacuitapenses traveling north since 2008 have paid an average of $3,000 for the services of a coyote. An explanation for this increase is the rising demand for coyotes, an unintended consequence of more stringent border enforcement measures. It follows that as demand for coyotes increases, they raise their prices.

In addition to the increasing amount being spent on trips to the United States, Tlacuitapenses are also changing how they are financing these trips. Of those that made their most recent trip between 2000 and 2007, 51.2 percent received the money to make the trip from their family and friends, mostly U.S.-based migrants. During this time, migrants also tapped their personal savings (16.3 percent) or obtained loans (25.6 percent) to finance their trip. After 2008, however, nearly three-fourths of undocumented Tlacuitapenses indicated borrowing money from U.S.-based friends and family. This increased reliance on U.S.-based relatives and friends to finance migration in recent years is perhaps not surprising, as U.S.-based Tlacuitapenses indicated steady or increasing wages in recent years.

In addition to higher coyote costs, the high physical risks associated with clandestine border crossings—another unintended consequence of enhanced U.S. border enforcement efforts—must be considered by potential migrants. Of the undocumented migrants in our sample who made their most recent trip to the United States between 2000 and 2007, each one had not only witnessed but personally experienced some type of violence en route to the border, whether perpetrated by the Mexican police, the Mexican army, coyotes, or U.S. Border Patrol agents. Undocumented migrants who had made their most recent trip to the United States since 2008 reported similar experiences. All of these migrants witnessed some kind of violence, and all but one personally experienced such acts.

We asked undocumented respondents who had made a trip to the United States since 2008 to identify the three most dangerous aspects of crossing the border without documents (see figure 2.16).

Figure 2.16 Worrisome Aspects of Unauthorized Border Crossing

More than one-third of respondents cited Mexican bandits (35.3 percent) while an equal number (35.3 percent) cited natural hazards as their foremost concern. A fear of drug traffickers was cited by 17.7 percent of migrants as their top concern. Previous research on Tlacuitapense migration before 2007 found the three most worrisome aspects of border crossing to be natural hazards (extreme temperatures in the deserts and mountains), followed by Mexican bandits and Border Patrol agents (Sisco and Hicken, 2009). The prevalence of these concerns is supported by the responses of the participants in our 2013 survey. Of respondents who had made their last trip to the United States before 2008, a plurality (38 percent) cited Mexican bandits as the most worrisome aspect of crossing the border. A smaller number of migrants (27.6 percent) cited natural hazards as their foremost concern while the third largest group of migrants (12.5 percent) cited Border Patrol agents as their top concern. Both groups of migrants, those who migrated after 2008 and those migrated before 2008, targeting Mexican bandits as a top concern illustrates the importance of non-state actors in influencing perceptions of border crossing dangers.

Previous research explained how Tlacuitapenses associated Mexican bandits or gangs with the drug-related violence in their country (Hicken, Fishbein, and Lisle, 2011). There also has been an increase in the number of Tlacuitapenses migrating after 2008 who explicitly indicated drug traffickers as the greatest border-crossing concern. Of those migrants who made a trip before 2008, only 4.2 percent reported drug traffickers as their greatest concern, compared to 17.7 percent of those who migrated after 2008. Data compiled by Human Rights Watch show 60,000 deaths related to drug trafficking in Mexico between 2006 and 2012 (Shoichet, 2013). Given this high death toll, and its concentration in Mexico's border states, it is not surprising that Tlacuitapenses migrating to the United States since 2008 were increasingly concerned about violence and organized crime in the borderlands. Awareness of natural hazards remained high, however. More than three-quarters (76.5 percent) of recent migrants cited extreme temperatures as one of their top three concerns. This concern is grounded in the shift in border crossings since the mid-1990s toward the central Arizona desert, where most clandestine crossings by Tlacuitapenses continue to be made (see below).

The displacement of U.S. Border Patrol as a top ranked concern for undocumented migrants after 2008 is a significant change in perceptions of the border crossing experience. Despite the lower ranking of Border Patrol as one of the most worrisome aspect of border crossing, Tlacuitapenses' migration decisions have been influenced by the ramp-up of border enforcement initiatives. As a consequence of concentrated border enforcement operations that were implemented along the California and Texas segments of the border beginning in 1994, Tlacuitapenses have exhibited a preference for crossing the border in Arizona since the mid-1990s. Despite heavy investment in border fortification efforts like physical fencing and electronic surveillance at the Arizona border since 2006, this section of the border in the harsh Arizona desert remains more porous than elsewhere. As a result, the coyote industry has become more concentrated on traveling through Arizona. Nevertheless, there is abundant evidence of the increased physical risks associated with crossing through that segment of the border. According to an article from The New York Times, of the 463 border-crossing deaths in 2012, the sector of the border near Tucson, Arizona accounted for the greatest number (Santos and Zemansky, 2013). Despite this elevated risk, figure 2.17 demonstrates that Tlacuitapense preference for Arizona has become stronger in recent years.

Figure 2.17   Location of Last Border Crossing

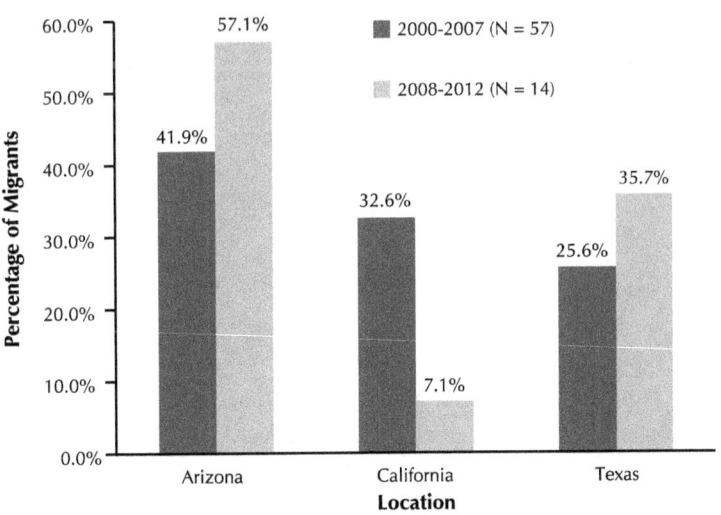

There also has been a sharp decline in crossings via the California-Mexico border. While about one-third of migrants crossed through the San Diego sector between 2000 and 2007, only 7.1 percent of our interviewees did so since 2008. In recent years, relatively fewer migrants have attempted entry through legal ports-of-entry, using false documents or hidden in vehicles. Of migrants who made their most recent trip between 2000 and 2007, 53.5 percent reported that they had passed through a legal checkpoint. This percentage decreased to 33.3 percent among migrants entering since 2008, as more migrants opted to cross through the Arizona desert.

This shift in mode of entry may be related to the Great Recession, which could have reduced the capacity of U.S.-based Tlacuitapenses to finance expensive ($5,000-6,000 U.S. or more) crossings made through a legal ports of entry, for which coyotes can charge much more. Previous research has shown that migrants entering through legal ports of entry are significantly more likely to avoid detection than migrants crossing through remote areas between legal ports-of-entry (Hicken, Fishbein, and Lisle, 2011).

Nevertheless, we found that despite this shift in mode in entry, Tlacuitapenses are still crossing the border with high rates of success. Of the undocumented migrants who made their most recent trip since 2008, eleven out of fourteen (78.6 percent) were able to cross the border without being apprehended even once. Despite being apprehended, the remaining three migrants were able to cross successfully on their second or subsequent attempt, on the same trip to the border, to yield an "eventual success" rate of 100 percent. Field studies of undocumented migration by our research team since 2005 have consistently found eventual success rates exceeding 90 percent, regardless of point of origin in Mexico. Among Tlacuitapense migrants whom we interviewed in 2013 whose most recent border-crossing attempt had occurred prior to 2008, 26.7 percent were apprehended on their first try and 90.3 percent were eventually successful in entering without detection. Among all interviewees who had migrated clandestinely to the United States, 26.4 percent were apprehended on their most recent trip to the border and 86.5 percent were able to enter without detection on their second or subsequent try (see figure 2.18).

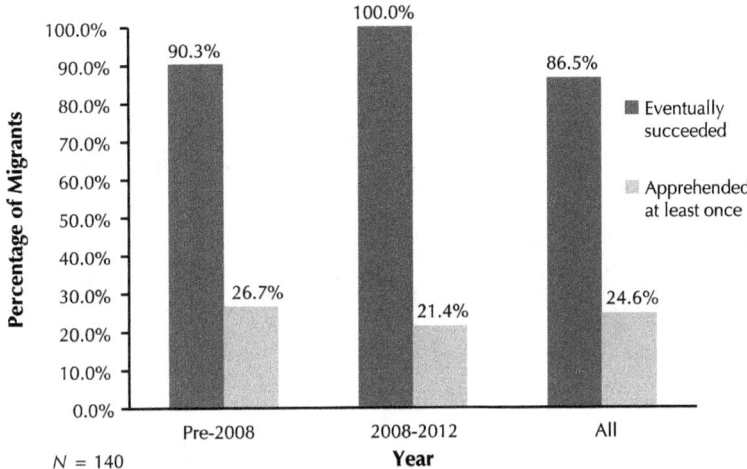

Figure 2.18 Apprehension Rates and Rates of Eventual Crossing Success

Oklahoma remained the preferred destination for Tlacuitapenses migrating between 2008 and 2012. Among undocumented migrants, the preference for Oklahoma increased from 58.1 percent between 2000 and 2007 to 66.7 percent since 2008. California destinations have been much less preferred in recent years. Between 2000 and 2007, about one out of five undocumented Tlacuitapenses migrants chose California as their destination, compared to just 6.7 percent since 2008. These preferences were consistent among all Tlacuitapenses migrants as well. 62.1 percent of all Tlacuitapenses making their most recent trip since 2008 chose to migrate to Oklahoma. This no doubt reflects not only the high cost of living in the Bay Area but also the severity of the Great Recession in California, which was more adversely impacted than Oklahoma. According to United States Census Bureau (2010), the cost of living in the San Francisco Bay Area is 164 percent the national average, while the cost of living in Oklahoma City is 91.7 percent. Furthermore, using data from the Bureau of Labor Statistics (2013b), there has been consistently higher unemployment rate for the Bay Area—6.2 percent as of April 2013—than in Oklahoma City (4.1 percent).

It follows that of the 5.2 percent of Tlacuitapenses indicated migrating to California since 2008, none migrated to Union City, CA, a traditional satellite community of Tlacuitapense migrants. Tlacuitapenses interviewed in Union City also highlighted this trend, reporting that due to the high costs of living in the Bay Area, more migrants choose a different destination when migrating or have moved out of Union City. We found evidence of this pattern in our data as well. Of Tlacuitapenses living in Union City at any time between 2008 and 2012, 30.8 percent had made the decision to move out of the Bay Area to somewhere else in the United States at the time of our fieldwork. It seems that just as the recession played a large role in Tlacuitapenses' settlement and return decisions between 2008 and 2012, it has been influential in the internal migration of Tlacuitapenses within the United States during that period as well.

CONCLUSION

We return to the question posed in our title: What matters most in migrants' decision making? In short, our results indicate that economic and social factors have a greater influence than policy factors in a Tlacuitapense's decision to settle in the United States or return to Mexico. While having a U.S. born child was a predictor of settlement, a combination of economic variables—wealth, job sector, and income—seems to play the most prominent role in settlement decisions. In terms of return, economic factors, namely a decline in wages, were the most important in a Tlacuitapense's decision to return.

Given that a decline in wages was the only statistically significant predictor of return for Tlacuitapenses between 2008 and 2012, we can be confident in attributing the rate of return primarily to the economic recession. While a majority of Tlacuitapenses (76.5 percent) have chosen to stay put in the United States and wait out the recession—likely due to economic comparisons they make between the United States and Mexico—we found the Tlacuitapense rate of return between 2008 and 2012 to be a 44 percent increase in the rate of return between 2003 and 2008.

Importantly, this finding represents a departure from prior research which indicated migrants, including Tlacuitapenses, were not "giving up" and returning to Mexico due to the economic recession. As a result, we must ask—why are we seeing this increase in return migration among Tlacuitapense migrants? Prior MMFRP research has documented the strategies that migrants living in the United States have utilized to face the economic realities of the Great Recession. Aguilar et al. (2010) found that Tunkaseño migrants—many of whom are undocumented—relied on their Tunkaseño social networks to find jobs and reduce living expenses in the United States (e.g. sharing meals or moving in together.) As a result of many Tunkaseño migrants being in the same position economically and in terms of documentation status, they were able to band together, even in the face of difficulties.

In communities with high proportionns of documented migrants, like Tlacuitapa, this type of solidarity may not occur, as those living without papers may feel isolated from the community. This feeling was expressed by an undocumented Tlacuitapense living in Union City, stating he avoids spending time with documented Tlacuitapenses because of their behavior towards those without papers. As a result, it may not be that Tlacuitapense returnees faced any graver economic realities than did Tunkaseños. However, undocumented Tlacuitapenses may be more likely to return to Mexico given their position in the community relative to those who are documented.

Nevertheless, it is important to highlight this return is not necessarily permanent, as almost seven out of ten returned migrants plan to go back to the United States in 2013. It follows that the idea of a "mass exodus" could be better described as simply an increase in temporary return migration. It will be essential to return to Tlacuitapa in the future in order to see if those expressing a desire to migrate once more to the United States actually did so or if the economically-induced rate of return will continue to increase.

With regard to policy factors, having legal status is the most statistically significant predictor of settlement in the United States. Nevertheless, this finding does not provide evidence of the efficacy of interior enforcement efforts in discouraging settlement or prompting returns to Mexico. Indeed, having been detained by immigration authorities, our independent variable measuring interior enforcement, was not a statistically significant predictor of settlement or return. In fact, several undocumented Tlacuitapenses whom we interviewed, in both Union City and Oklahoma

City, related experiences of amicable interactions with local police officers and immigration officials. Diego, a returned migrant who had lived in El Paso, Texas, described his experience of working to construct a segment of border fence for immigration officers. He recalled: "I had the opportunity to talk to some of them [and they] were good people. I never had any problems with anyone." Such evidence challenges the conventional wisdom that tougher immigration enforcement away from the border area (the "attrition through [interior] enforcement" approach) is an effective way of prompting returns to Mexico.

Other policy factors, like expectations of a future legalization program, also were not found to be statistically significant predictors of the decision to settle or return. However, the lack of emphasis that migrants place on potential legalization can possibly be attributed to frustration with the stagnation of comprehensive immigration reform over the past decade. Rocio, an undocumented migrant living in Oklahoma, described her frustration with U.S. politics: "Obama won and I cried like a madwoman. But then I became cold and thought, 'What do I gain if they are not going to give us anything?'" This frustration, coupled with the lack of knowledge reported by our interviewees regarding important policy initiatives like DACA, suggest an overall weakness of policy factors in migrants' decision-making processes. However, one limitation to this study comes from the high rates of documentation status and the corresponding low-rates of eligibility for DACA among members of the Tlacuitapense community. Consequently, further research in other populations having higher proportions of unauthorized migrants is needed to determine if policy developments like DACA play a larger role in these communities.

Prior research has indicated the limits of immigration policy in controlling migrant stocks and flows—whether due to ambiguous policy intents or unintended policy outcomes (Cornelius and Tsuda, 2004). Often, the imperfect implementation of policies, as evidenced by the positive interactions between undocumented migrants and law enforcement mentioned above, also play a role in the ineffectiveness of policy. As divisive debates over comprehensive immigration reform continue, our research underscores the need for policymakers to understand these realities.

Finally, policymakers must understand the complex process that results in decisions to settle in the United States or return to Mexico. Importantly, our research indicates that restrictive policies have largely been ineffective at encouraging undocumented migrants to return to Mexico, which is largely a function of social and especially economic variables in a migrant's life. It follows that policymakers should shift their attention to policies that would promote immigrant integration and ensure that future flows of migrants from Mexico will be predominantly legal.

REFERENCES

Alarcón, R., FitzGerald, D.S., and Muse-Orlinoff, L. (2011). Introduction: Tlacuitapa Revisited. In D.S. FitzGerald, R. Alarcon, and L. Muse-Orlinoff (Eds.), Recession Without Borders: Mexican Migrants Confront the Economic Downturn (1-14). La Jolla, CA: Center for Comparative Immigration Studies, UCSD.

Batalova, J. and Mittelstadt, M. (2012). Relief from Deportation: Demographic Profile of the DREAMers Potentially Eligible under the Deferred Action Policy. Washington, DC: Migration Policy Institute. Retrieved from: http://www.migrationpolicy.org/pubs/fs24_deferredaction.pdf

Bhatt, W., and Roberts, B.R. (2012). "Forbidden Return": Return Migration in the Age of Restriction. Journal of Immigrant and Refugee Studies, 10(2): 162–183.

Bureau of Labor Statistics. (2013a). Unemployment rate by major worker group, February 2013. Retrieved from: http://www.bls.gov/opub/ted/2013/ted_20130312.htm

Bureau of Labor Statistics. (2013b). Metropolitan Area Employment and Unemployment, April 2013. Retrieved from http://www.bls.gov/news.release/pdf/metro.pdf

Cabrera-Hernández, J., Hall, A., de Anda J., Romero, D.R., and Saldaña, R. (2011). Coping with Hard Times in El Norte. In D.S . FitzGerald, R. Alarcon, and L. Muse-Orlinoff (Eds.), Recession Without Borders: Mexican Migrants Confront the Economic Downturn (95-109). La Jolla, CA: Center for Comparative Immigration Studies, UCSD.

Cornelius, W.A. and Tsuda, T. (2004). Controlling Immigration: The Limits of Government Intervention. In W.A. Cornelius, T. Tsuda, P. L. Martin, and J.F. Hollifield (eds.), Controlling Immigration: A Global Perspective (2nd ed.) (2-48). Stanford, CA: Stanford University Press.

Durand, J., and Massey, D.S. (2004). Crossing the Border: Research from the Mexican Migration Project. New York, NY: The Russell Sage Foundation.

García, A., Griesbach, K., Andrade, J., González, C., and Yrizar Barbosa, G. (2011). Pressure from the Inside: The Subnational Politics of Immigration. In D.S . FitzGerald, R. Alarcon, and L. Muse-Orlinoff (Eds.), Recession Without Borders: Mexican Migrants Confront the Economic Downturn (37-61). La Jolla, CA: Center for Comparative Immigration Studies, UCSD.

García, A. and Barreno A. (2007). Tunkaseño Settlement in the United States. In W. Cornelius, D. FitzGerald, and P. L. Fischer (eds.), Mayan Journeys: The New Migration from Yucatan to the United States (115–139). La Jolla, CA: Center for Comparative Immigration Studies, UCSD.

Hoefer, M., Rytina, N., and Baker, B.C. (2012). Estimates of the Unauthorized Immigrant Population Residing in the United States: January 2011. Retrieved fromhttp://www.dhs.gov/xlibrary/assets/statistics/publications/ois_ill_pe_2011.pdf

Hicken, J., Fishbein, J., and Lisle, J. (2011). U.S. Border Enforcement: The Limits of Physical and Remote Deterrence of Unauthorized Migration. In D. S. FitzGerald, R. Alarcón, and L. Muse-Orlinoff (Eds.), Recession Without Borders: Mexican Migrants Confront the Economic Downturn (17-35). La Jolla, CA: Center for Comparative Immigration Studies, UCSD.

Jarvis, J., Ponce, A., Rodríguez, S., and García, L.C. (2009).The Dynamics of Migration: Who Migrates? Who Stays? Who Settles Abroad? In W.A. Cornelius, D. FitzGerald, and S. Borger (Eds.), Four Generations of Nortenos: New Research from the Cradle of Mexican Migration (1-38). La Jolla, CA: Center for Comparative Immigration Studies, University of Califoria, San Diego.

Landsberg, M. (2012). Obama hits Romney on "self-deportation" of illegal immigrants. Los Angeles Times. Retrieved from http://articles.latimes.com/2012/oct/17/news/la-pn-obama-romney-self-deportation-20121016

López, M.H., and Taylor, P. (2012). Latino Voters in the 2012 Election. Retrieved from http://www.pewhispanic.org/2012/11/07/latino-voters-in-the-2012-election/

Marcelli, E. A., and Cornelius, W. A. (2001). The Changing Profile of Mexican Migrants to the United States: New Evidence from California and Mexico. Latin American Research Review, 36(3):105–131. doi:10.2307/2692122

McKeown, A. (1999). Transnational Chinese Families and Chinese Exclusion, 1875-1943. Journal of American Ethnic History, 18(2): 73-110.

Migration Policy Institute. (2013). 2011 American Community Survey and Census Data on the Foreign Born by State. Retrieved from: http://www.migrationinformation.org/datahub/acscensus.cfm

Pew Hispanic Center. (2013). A Nation of Immigrants. Retrieved from: http://www.pewhispanic.org/2013/01/29/a-nation-of-immigrants/

Puentes, V., Hong, R. and Valencia, E. (2011) Deciding to Migrate. In D. S. FitzGerald, R. Alarcón, and L. Muse-Orlinoff (Eds.), Recession Without Borders: Mexican Migrants Confront the Economic Downturn (63-73). La Jolla, CA: Center for Comparative Immigration Studies, UCSD.

Rendall, M., Brownell, P., and Kups, S. (2011). Declining Return Migration From the United States to Mexico in the Late-2000s Recession: A Research Note. Demography, 48(3): 1049–1058.

Redburn, S., Reuter, P., and Majmundar M., eds. (2011) Budgeting for Immigration Enforcement: Report of the Committee on Estimating Costs of Immigration Enforcement in the Department of Justice. Washington, DC: National Academies Press.

Reyes, B. I. (2004). Changes in Trip Duration for Mexican Immigrants to the United States. Population Research and Policy Review, 23(3): 235–257.

Riosmena, F. (2004). Return Versus Settlement Among Undocumented Mexican Migrants, 1980 to 1996. In J. Durand and D. S. Massey (eds.), Crossing the Border (265-280). New York: The Russell Sage Foundation.

Santos, F., and Zemansky, R. (2013). Immigrant Death Rate Rises on Illegal Crossings. The New York Times. Retrieved from: http://www.nytimes.com/2013/05/21/us/immigrant-death-rate-rises-on-illegal-crossings.html

Shoichet, C. E. (2013.). A grisly crime surges into spotlight as Mexico shifts drug war strategy. CNN. Retrieved from: http://www.cnn.com/2013/03/27/world/americas/mexico-violence/index.html

Sisco, J. and Hicken, J. (2009). Is U.S. Border Enforcement Working? In W. A. Cornelius, D. FitzGerald, and S. Borger (Eds.), Four Generations of Nortenos: New Research from the Cradle of Mexican Migration (41-76). La Jolla, CA: Center for Comparative Immigration Studies, UCSD.

Suro, R., and Zenteno, R. (2012). Overview: Mexican Migration Beyond the Downturn and Deportations. Retrieved from http://www.migrationmonitor.com/1-article/

United States Census Bureau. (2012). Cost of Living Index—Selected Urban Areas [Data file]. Retrieved from: http://www.census.gov/compendia/statab/cats/prices/consumer_price_indexes_cost_of_living_index.html

U.S. Citizenship and Immigration Services. (2013a). Consideration of Deferred Action for Childhood Arrivals Process. Retrieved from http://www.uscis.gov/childhoodarrivals

U.S. Citizenship and Immigration Services. (2013b). Data on Individual Applications and Petition, May 2013. Retrieved from: http://www.uscis.gov/USCIS/Resources/Reports%20and%20Studies/Immigration%20Forms%20Data/Static_files/2013-0516%20DACA%20Monthly%20Report%2005-09-13.pdf

Waldinger, R. D., and Lim, N. (2009). Connectivity and Collectivity: Immigrant Involvement in Homeland Politics. Retrieved from: http://works.bepress.com/roger_waldinger/31

Resumen

¿ASENTARSE O REGRESAR?, QUÉ IMPORTA MÁS EN LAS DECISIONES DE LOS MIGRANTES

HILLARY S. KOSNAC, YARAZEL MEJORADO, SARAH M. DAVIDSON, MOISÉS MARROQUÍN AND CELESTINO NAZARIO

El tema más polémico en el 2013 -- al igual que en 2006 y 2007 -- sobre la reforma migratoria, es el camino adecuado para la obtención de ciudadanía del gran número de migrantes indocumentados que viven en Estados Unidos. En los últimos años, este país ha experimentado una severa recesión económica al tiempo que ha implementado políticas de reforzamiento internas cada vez más restrictivas. En medio de estas condiciones, sin embargo, no ha habido ninguna mella significativa en el tamaño de la población indocumentada. Este panorama aparentemente contradictorio, es el que se trata de aclarar a través de este estudio, con el uso de un análisis de regresión múltiple junto con entrevistas cualitativas.

A la fecha, existen una gran cantidad de investigaciones sobre la decisión de emigrar, pero hay menos interesadas en los factores que influyen en las decisiones de los migrantes a establecerse en Estados Unidos o regresar a México. Este estudio explora la importancia de la economía, de las políticas de inmigración y de los factores sociales en la toma de decisiones de los Tlacuitapenses para establecerse en los Estados Unidos o regresar a México.

Entre los hallazgos, se pudo saber que para aquellos que se establecen en los Estados Unidos, las decisiones con mayor influencia se toman bajo una combinación de factores económicos - nivel de riqueza, sector laboral, y salarios fijos-. Además de los aspectos económicos, algunos aspectos sociales resultan de importancia secundaria, tales como tener un hijo nacido en EE.UU.

Se analizó también el proceso de toma de decisiones de los migrantes, particularmente de quienes han optado por regresar a Tlacuitapa desde 2008, en esta tarea encontramos que los factores económicos como la disminución de salarios, tuvo el papel con mayor influencia al momento de decidir regresar.

Nuestros datos permitieron conocer un aumento de la tasa de retorno a Tlacuitapa, en comparación con estudios previos llevados a cabo por MMFRP en la misma comunidad. El único factor con valor predictivo estadísticamente significativo, para determinar el regreso desde el año 2008, fue la disminución de los salarios. Teniendo esto en cuenta, podemos confiar en atribuir este incremento a los efectos de la recesión económica. No obstante, debe entenderse que este fenómeno puede no ser permanente; ya que, la mayoría de estos inmigrantes manifestaron tener planes de regresar a los Estados Unidos en un futuro próximo.

Al examinar las motivaciones de los migrantes asentados y de retorno, encontramos algunas similitudes interesantes, a saber, la disminuida importancia de los factores políticos. Con respecto a estos, el factor con mayor valor predictivo estadísticamente significativo, es tener un estatus migratorio legal. Sin embargo, este hallazgo no constituye una prueba sobre la eficacia de los esfuerzos en la aplicación de políticas de reforzamiento internas que desalienten en ingreso a USA o inciten el regreso a México. Otros factores políticos, como la expectativa de un futuro programa de legalización, tampoco resultaron tener valor predictivo estadísticamente significativos en la decisión de asentarse o volver. La falta de conocimiento entre los entrevistados, sobre iniciativas políticas importantes como la Acción Diferida, sugiere una debilidad general de los factores políticos en los procesos de toma de decisiones los migrantes.

La relativa falta de importancia que los tlacuitapenses otorgan a las leyes y políticas de inmigración de Estados Unidos, desafía el conocimiento convencional de que mientras más dura sea la vigilancia fronteriza y más duros los controles migratorios interiores, se logra de manera eficaz disuadir a los inmigrantes no autorizados a ingresar al país, o a intentar hacerlo. Es importante destacar, que nuestra investigación indica que las políticas restrictivas han sido en gran medida ineficaces para alentar a los inmigrantes indocumentados a regresar a México, tal decisión la toman los migrantes en función de variables sociales y económicas en particular, que tienen efecto en sus vidas cotidianas.

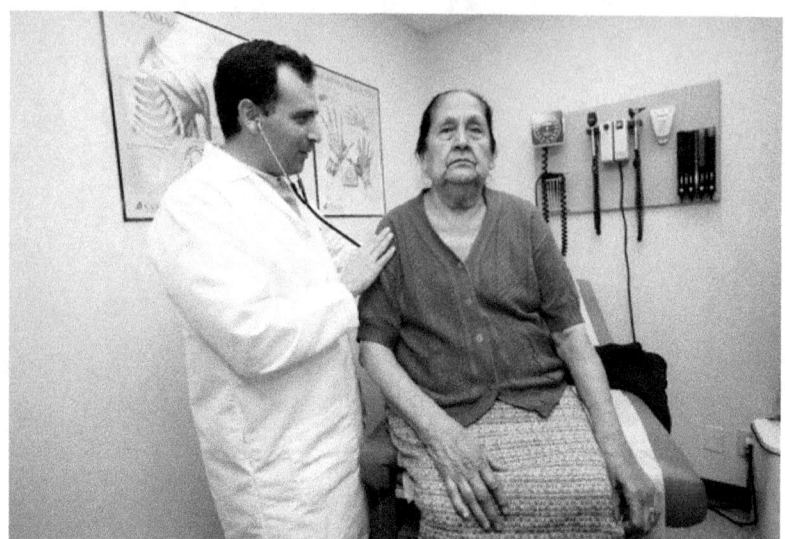
Immigrant woman being examined in a California community clinic. (Photo by Associated Press)

3   Fear and Other Barriers to Accessing Health Care Services for Tlacuitapenses

Dinorah L. Sánchez, Catherine Elizabeth Benson, and Miriam Adriana Arredondo Cervantes

> *When we feel like that, when we're sick, we prefer to stay at home … I prefer, for the flu or something, to take care of myself at home, to avoid going to the hospital. Because you get scared, the bills, the not knowing English, you don't know anything.*
> Beatriz, a 35-year-old undocumented woman in Oklahoma

According to the Pew Hispanic Center, of the 40 million migrants currently in the United States, more than 11 million live without documentation – 58 percent of whom are of Mexican origin. Under the Obama administration, deportations increased over 30 percent, and surveys have found that one of every three Latino migrants personally knows someone who has been detained or deported within the preceding twelve months (Pew Hispanic Center, 2013). This high rate of detainment leads to elevated fear among undocumented immigrants.

While the comprehensive immigration reform bill proposed in 2013 contains a path to legalization, even if enacted the law would not repair all issues of access to health care services. Those undocumented migrants who would qualify to adjust their status would have a "registered provisional immigrant" status and would be required to wait at least ten years before qualifying to apply for legal permanent residency. During that time, they would be ineligible to access federal public benefits, such as Medicaid. Although they would be forced to purchase health insurance or pay the tax penalty under the Affordable Care Act, they will not be eligible for any of the tax credits or discounts available to low-income workers (National Immigration Law Center, 2013).

Migrants, both documented and undocumented, often experience various challenges to accessing health care services. In addition to those imposed by federal law, the barriers include fear due to immigration status, lack of insurance, lack of finances, and language difficulties (Hacker et al., 2011, 2012; Heyman, Nuñez and Talavera, 2009; Wong-Kim et al., 2009; Fuentes-Afflick and Hessol, 2009; Documét and Sharma, 2004). After Heyman, Nuñez and Talavera (2009), we define the fear barrier as encompassing a generalized fear of authorities, such as being arrested when traveling to access health care services, or fear of deportation due to immigration status. We add to this definition fear of costs, fear of language problems, and fear of discrimination, all of which were reported during our fieldwork and are consistent with previous studies (Maldonado et al., 2013; Cristancho et al., 2008).

This chapter focuses on fear and other barriers to accessing health care services, including language, costs, and discrimination. We hypothesized that language, cost, and fear due to migration status lead undocumented Tlacuitapenses to access fewer health care services than their documented counterparts. Consistent with previous studies, we argue that undocumented migrants face greater barriers to health care than authorized migrants; more specifically, the undocumented are more likely to report fear due to their status, perceived discrimination, language and financial barriers as reasons to deter or delay seeking care (Hacker et al., 2011, 2012; Heyman, Nuñez and Talavera, 2009; Wong-Kim et al., 2009; Fuentes-Afflick and Hessol, 2009; Documét and Sharma, 2004).

By examining the barriers to health care for this population, we hope to illuminate areas in which policy interventions could be beneficial. The United States has much work to do creating a just immigration system. However, smaller policy changes could improve the health of undocumented migrants, while lessening their economic impact on the health care system. We also hope that our study helps health care practitioners who work with immigrant patients in hospitals, community clinics, and private practices, as well as immigrant advocates.

LITERATURE REVIEW

Various scholars have investigated the impact of documentation status on access to health care services. Vargas Bustamante et al. (2012), found that documented Mexican migrants are 76 percent more likely to report seeing a doctor in the past year than undocumented migrants. Most of this difference can be accounted for by socio-demographic factors including age, education, employment, insurance status and income. However, 12 percent of the difference in this study remains unexplained, and the authors suggest that this could relate to deportation fears, availability of safety nets and a lack of familiarity with the health care system.

The results from a study conducted by Ortega and colleagues (2007), indicated that among all Latinos surveyed, undocumented migrants are the least likely to report having a usual source of care. Of the Mexican participants, both undocumented migrants and naturalized citizens reported the highest rates of barriers to care in the past year, whereas for other Latinos, it was U.S.-born citizens who had the highest proportions. Regardless of status, all Latino migrants had the lowest mean number of health care visits in the last year. Latino undocumented migrants had the highest rates of reporting difficulty understanding their physicians and feeling they were discriminated against. Mexican migrants in general had lower rates of having a usual care provider, higher rates of problems accessing care in the last year, fewer physician visits (including emergency department visits), and were more likely to report that they would have received better care if they were from a different race or ethnicity.

Fuentes-Afflick and Hessol (2009) found that undocumented women surveyed in the San Francisco area were less likely to have medical insurance than documented and U.S. citizen women. The undocumented women were also less likely to have received health care services in the year prior to being surveyed.

Previous studies have investigated the effect of fear on access to health care. Berk and Shur (2001) looked specifically at the impact of fear on the undocumented population's access to care. Among the undocumented migrants surveyed in El Paso, Los Angeles and Fresno, 39 percent responded that they feared accessing services due to their status. Out of those who expressed fear, 14 percent reported deterring health care services within the last year, compared to 3 percent of those who did not express fear. Another study (Cavazos-Rehg, Zayas, and Spitznagel 2007) showed that 39 percent of Latino undocumented migrants expressed concern in seeking health care services due to fear of deportation.

Dang, Giordano and Kim (2012), conducted a qualitative study of undocumented Latinos with HIV in Texas. Most participants were diagnosed in a hospital after receiving emergency care. In addition to the stigma of the disease and language barriers, participants reported both experienced and perceived barriers due to their undocumented status. Lack of identification and proof of income made it difficult to comply with paperwork requirements for available health services. Some participants reported deterring care due to the inability to get time off work for medical appointments. Respondents also reported fear that utilizing health care services would result in deportation. Additionally, patients feared that being deported to their home country would lead to not only a loss of income, but also loss of their HIV treatment. The study found that fear of deportation and lack of awareness of available services led to delayed diagnosis and treatment among participants. This delay occurs in spite of several state programs available to all HIV patients in Texas, regardless of status.

Following local Immigration and Customs Enforcement (ICE) raids in Everett, Massachusetts, Hacker and colleagues (2011, 2012), investigated how these well-publicized events affected health care access for migrant patients. The research was conducted in response to reports that migrants were missing their health care appointments following the raids. In the first study, researchers conducted focus groups with migrant participants, the majority of whom were undocumented. Surprisingly, most had health insurance and had seen a doctor in the last year. Four major themes were found among the participants: fear of deportation, perceived collaboration between ICE and local law enforcement, concern of being reported to ICE officials due to documentation collected for insurance and health care services, and effect on migrants' physical and emotional well-being. Other concerns mentioned included the high cost of health care services and discrimination based on race and ethnicity (Hacker et al., 2011). In a follow-up study, health care practitioners, including primary care and emergency department providers, were surveyed. 40 percent of respondents reported that ICE activities had negative impacts on their patients' health. Health care practitioners reported that the negative impact was due both to the effect that fear of deportation had on patients' emotional health and to the interruption of health care caused by that fear. Fear of deportation led some patients to avoid care due to fear that receiving care and applying for available health benefits would lead to exposure of their documentation status (Hacker et al., 2012).

By interviewing patients in the emergency department, Maldonado et al. (2013) sought to establish the lower boundary of fear of undocumented migrants seeking health care services. Twelve percent of undocumented participants expressed fear of going to the hospital, among that group 71 percent citing fear of being deported, and 16 percent reporting fear of not receiving medical care. Of the undocumented patients surveyed, 16 percent reported that undocumented patients are treated differently than other patients. Among these interviewees 41 percent of whom stated they receive less respect or lower standard of care, while 37 percent cited language barriers as a reason for the inadequate care, and 16 percent reported longer wait times for the undocumented.

Wong-Kim et al. (2009) conducted a study of undocumented women in California and Texas where they note that "language barriers, lack of knowledge about the U.S. health care system, and fear of detection by immigration authorities" (p. S65) are barriers to health care services for undocumented migrants. Andersen et al. (1981) also found that language was a significant barrier when Latinos reported not seeing a doctor because of the absence of Spanish-speaking personnel when seeking health care in hospitals. Documentation status was not collected in their study. Likewise, Quesada (1976) found that the lack of bilingual medical services and personnel lead Mexican-Americans with limited English abilities to postpone or avoid needed health care.

Other studies have focused on other barriers for undocumented migrants in accessing care, such as high costs, discrimination, and hostile attitudes (Cleveland and Ihara, 2012). Cristancho et al. (2008) identify cost as barrier to health care, with interviewees expressing concern about the high cost of health care services and the lack of health care financing plans. This study also found language to be a barrier. The primary language concern was not English itself. Instead, respondents reported a lack of knowledge about medical terminology, which resulted in a poor understanding of their health problems and inadequate treatment. In a study of Latinos living in Southwest Pennsylvania, Documét and Sharma (2004) found that participants refrained from using health care services as much as possible after having negative experiences, such as discrimination and conflict due to language, cultural, or financial barriers.

USE OF HEALTH CARE SERVICES BY TLACUITAPENSES LIVING IN THE UNITED STATES

This chapter focuses on health care services accessed in the United States; therefore, we limit our study population to Tlacuitapenses who have U.S. residence experience. This produced a sample of 170 interviewees, 22 percent of whom were undocumented. For purposes of this analysis, we define documented Tlacuitapenses as legal permanent residents, naturalized U.S. citizens, and those born in the United States. Undocumented Tlacuitapenses are those who entered the United States clandestinely or lost their documented status. The gender of our respondents was almost evenly distributed, with 53 percent males and 47 percent females. Slightly more than half (52 percent) of our interviewees currently live in Oklahoma, 28 percent in California's Bay Area, 5 percent in Texas, 4 percent in Illinois, and 11 percent in other U.S. locations. For our analysis we focus on interviewees living in Oklahoma and California, since those are the states where the majority of Tlacuitapenses reside. All other locations are grouped together.

According to our survey results, undocumented respondents are less likely to have a primary care provider than documented respondents. Sixty-nine percent of the latter reported having a primary care provider, compared to 64 percent of those without papers (figure 3.1). Respondents in California are more likely to report having a primary care provider than those living in Oklahoma. In California 77 percent reported having a primary care provider, versus only 58 percent in Oklahoma, and 69 percent for all other locations (figure 3.2).

Figure 3.1 Tlacuitapenses with Primary Health Provider in the United States by Documentation Status

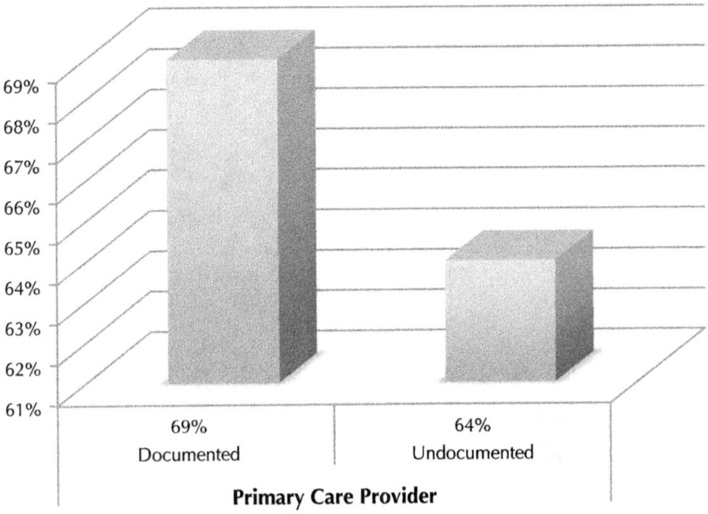

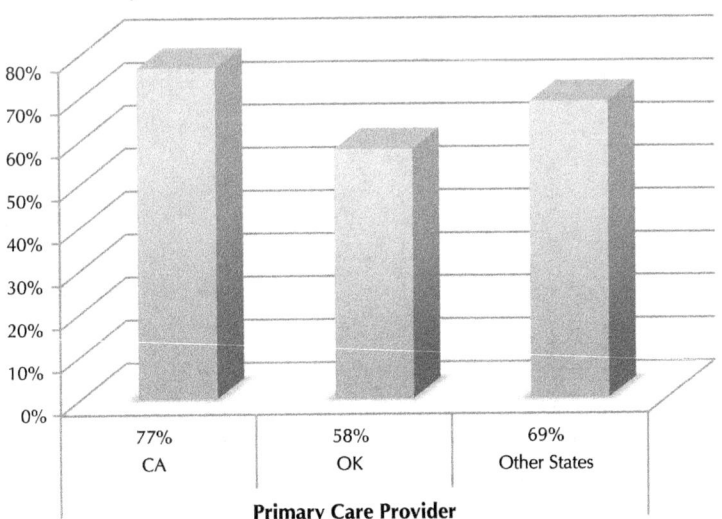

Figure 3.2 Tlacuitapenses with Primary Health Provider in the United States by Location

In case of an urgent medical matter, undocumented migrants are more likely to receive care at hospitals than documented Tlacuitapenses. While only 38 percent of the latter went to hospitals if they had an urgent medical matter, 46 percent of the former went to hospitals (figure 3.3). Migrants with papers are 7 percent more likely than those without to visit a doctor or clinic. Participants who did not see a health professional used home remedies, self-medicated, or did nothing when responding to an urgent medical matter. In California, 60 percent of Tlacuitapenses visit a hospital for an urgent medical matter, compared to 57 percent in Oklahoma, and 32 percent in other states.

Figure 3.3 Types of Health Care Facilities Used by Tlacuitapenses with Urgent Medical Matters by Documentation

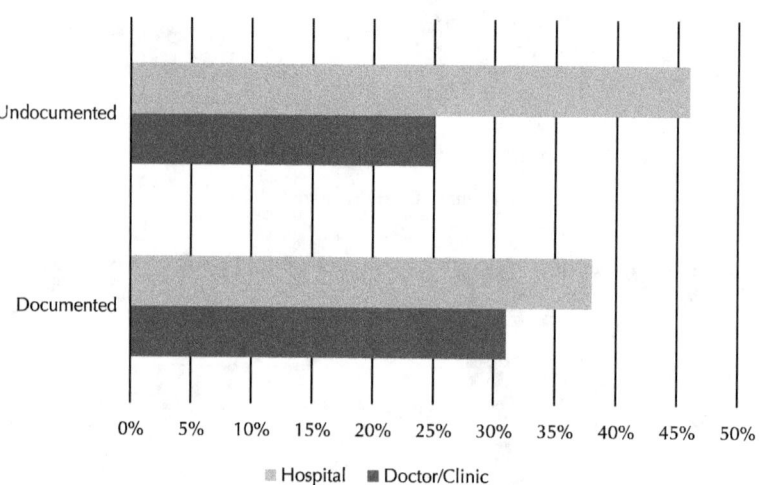

Our study also found that undocumented migrants are less likely to have received health care services in the past 12 months. While 60 percent of those with papers received health services in the past year, only 50 percent of those without papers received services (figure 3.4). In California, 60 percent of respondents reported receiving health care services in the past year, compared to only 56 percent of those in Oklahoma and 64 percent in other states. Moreover, only 18 percent of undocumented migrants reported taking medications, compared with 35 percent of documented respondents.

Figure 3.4 Tlacuitapenses' Use of Health Care Services Within the Past 12 Months by Documentation

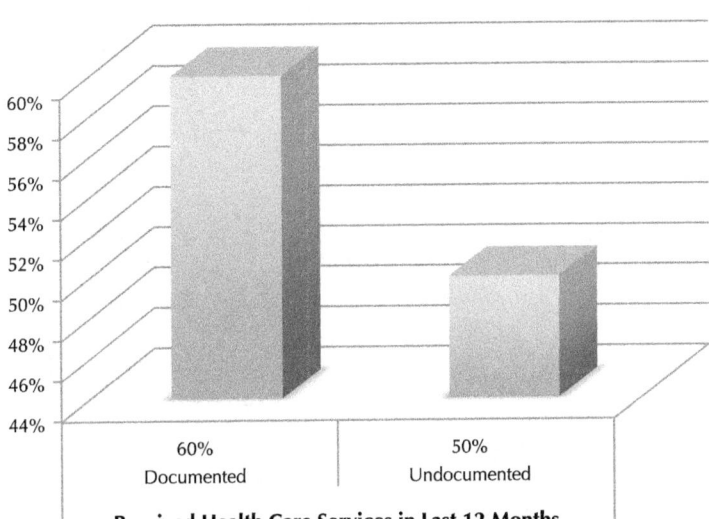

FEAR AS A BARRIER TO ACCESSING HEALTH CARE
Fear Due to Immigration Status

Undocumented migrants were more likely to report they did not go to the doctor because they were afraid of revealing their own or a family member's immigration status. Thirty-five percent of undocumented Tlacuitapenses responded they were afraid, compared to only 7 percent of documented Tlacuitapenses (figure 3.5).

Figure 3.5 Tlacuitapenses Reported Fear to Seek Health Care Services Due to Status

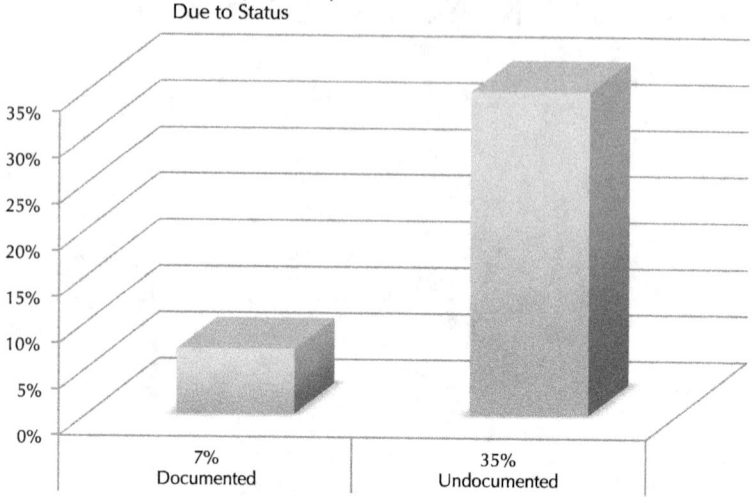

We used multiple regression analysis to determine the relative importance of wealth, education, English abilities, gender, age, location within the United States, and immigration status as predictors of fear to seek health care. Documentation status was the solely factor found to be statistically significant in reporting such a fear (table 3.1).

Table 3.1. Determinants of Being Afraid to Seek Health Care Services: Multiple Regression Analysis

	Model 1	Model 2
Documented/Undocumented	-2.031**	-2.049**
Wealth		-0.317
Education		0.075
Speaks English		-0.181
Male		0.015
Age		0.038
Living in California		0.431
Living in Oklahoma		0.758
N	103	90
R^2	0.099	0.109

Fear rooted in immigration status also emerged during our qualitative interviews. Alberto,[1] a 36 year-old migrant with experience in Oklahoma, reported not going to the doctor while living in Oklahoma due to his undocumented status. He was afraid of revealing his status and had feared that he would not be treated well. However, after eventually learning more about other clinics and spending more time in the United States, Alberto explained:

> Yes, when I went the first few times [to the U.S.] I was younger and afraid of everything and nervous. But now everything is easier because I matured and learned that they weren't going to do anything to me, and I started to not be afraid of things, of the hospital and of going to work - I just opened up and wasn't afraid of anything.

Delia, a 61-year-old living between Tlacuitapa and Oklahoma, has been a U.S. legal permanent resident for almost five years. Although she is documented, her son is living in the United States without papers. Delia shared that she and her husband often forgo accessing health care services because they fear it will negatively affect her son. The most recent time she became sick in Oklahoma, Delia decided not to go to the hospital and instead self-medicated with medications she had brought from Mexico. Like many Tlacuitapenses, before she leaves Mexico, Delia always ensures she has a three-month supply of all her prescriptions, as well as any other medications she anticipates needing if she happens to get ill while in Oklahoma. She stated that she prefers to come prepared, not only to avoid putting her son at risk, but also because of the cost and to avoid dealing with the U.S. health care system.

Beatriz, a 35 year-old undocumented migrant living in Oklahoma, also spoke of a constant fear due to her undocumented status. She has heard of people being deported from the hospital and is therefore afraid to go. Still, when she and her daughters had medical emergencies, she said she had no choice but to seek health care services in the dreaded emergency room.

---

1. All names mentioned in this chapter have been changed to protect the identity of our interviewees.

Beatriz summed it up: "We have to limit ourselves and avoid going to a hospital -- for fear of not knowing English, that they won't treat you, of the bills, of not wanting to owe anything."

Fear Due to of Cost of Health Services

During an interview while visiting Tlacuitapa, Lucia, a naturalized U.S. citizen living in Chicago, said she is afraid of accessing health care services because she does not know what her insurance will cover and how much the treatments will ultimately cost her. Her insurance pays a percentage of her charges, but she does not know the exact amount she will have to pay until the bill arrives. Due to a prior colonoscopy procedure, Lucia is currently in debt and fears going into more debt with additional health care services. As reported above, Beatriz also says she is afraid of going to the hospital because she is afraid of the bills and being in debt, stating "we don't want owe, we want to be in good standing."

Fear Due to Language Problems

Among Beatriz's many fears, foremost is related to language difficulties – the fear not being understood. Beatriz spoke about her need to take her daughter to the hospital yet she could not do so because she did not have an English speaker to accompany her and translate. In one instance, her brother was not be able to help her translate at the hospital and instead took them to Dr. Tran, who, though Vietnamese, speaks some Spanish and treats many Spanish-speaking patients. Although Dr. Tran is viewed as a trusted source of health care by many of our interviewees in Oklahoma, Beatriz is unsatisfied with his services due to his inability to communicate properly.

> He speaks two or three words in Spanish. All he says is 'shot, shot', that it's an infection, that's all. He never ever gives a good diagnosis. So, one goes there out of necessity, but not because we trust him.

Still, she admits that if she has an urgent medical matter for herself or her children and she has no one to translate for her, she would rather go to Dr. Tran than to the hospital.

Fear of Discrimination

Alberto spoke of fear of discrimination as a barrier to accessing health services. He fears being turned away because he is Mexican. He reported that after an experience of being refused care, he became afraid of being rejected yet another time.

> I remember going with my cousin. He was Chicano and he spoke English. They asked him for my identification. A nurse said my identification was fake but I told her it's the one they gave us at work. She said we had no insurance and that they couldn't help me. I was rejected.

After this experience Alberto feared accessing health care services and once stayed in his house, unable to work, for nine days with a high fever until he eventually felt better.

OTHER PERCEIVED BARRIERS TO ACCESSING HEALTH CARE

The Language Barrier

In our survey undocumented migrants reported greater language barriers when accessing health care than their documented counterparts. Respondents without papers were 6 percent more likely to report difficulty understanding their doctors than those with papers (figure 3.6). Of respondents who answered that they spoke little or no English, just over half reported trouble understanding his or her doctor. When asked about the translation services they received, only 30 percent of respondents used the clinic staff and 9 percent used a professional translator. Over 44 percent of respondents answered they used an adult relative to help with translation and 9 percent used a relative of minor age. In qualitative interviews we discovered that the "adult relatives" mentioned by our survey respondents actually included friends, coworkers, and supervisors as well. In sum, 61 percent of our interviewees had to provide their own translators; professionals provided only 39 percent of the translations.

Figure 3.6 Tacuitapenses With Difficulties Understanding Their Physician During Last Visit

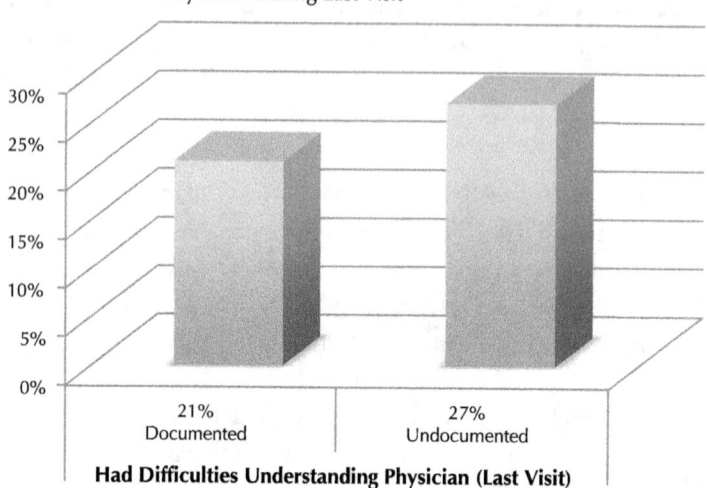

Had Difficulties Understanding Physician (Last Visit)

Language as a barrier to health care services was a common theme in our qualitative interviews. Alberto told us he had avoided receiving health care services because he believed clinic staff would not be able to understand him. When he became ill and unable to work, his only option was to stay home and wait until his health improved. Once his friends and coworkers told him of a clinic where the staff speak Spanish, he visited that clinic for health care services from that point on. He also mentioned Dr. Tran as an alternative to hospitals. Alberto said that physicians in hospitals only speak English, which he had difficulty understanding, and therefore he felt he was not paid as much attention by the staff. "I did feel rejected," he recalled, "by the güeras, the gabachas [non-Spanish-speaking white women] who would treat us."

Estéban told us about forgoing treatment for an occupational injury. The day a nail from an old nail gun went through his hand, his supervisor took him to the hospital and translated for him. However, when it was time for his follow-up appointment, his supervisor was no longer available or willing to take him. Estéban felt that there was no point in returning to the hospital since he would not be able to explain anything to the physician or understand any instructions.

Financial Barriers

In our qualitative interviews, many respondents reported the cost of health care as a major barrier to accessing it. Alicia is a 55-year-old naturalized U.S. citizen currently living in Texas who was interviewed while visiting Tlacuitapa. She reported that high costs kept her from accessing necessary health care services. Alicia's diabetes necessitates a regular eye exam but the cost of the exam is prohibitively high. In addition, she reported developing a rash as a possible side effect of her medications, but does not want to return to her physician simply because she is unable to afford the $120 bill. She also believes that she might have thyroid problems in addition to her other health ailments but cannot afford to get the necessary tests to have her questions resolved. Alicia has been able to arrange a regular payment plan with her primary care provider at the hospital for expensive procedures, but she cannot make arrangements with specialists. She believes that if the specialists had Spanish-speaking staff she might be better able to arrange payment plans.

Estéban talked about his struggles in accessing health care for work injuries. He commented that when employees are not able to prove that an injury occurred while working it is difficult to come up with the money to pay out of pocket for treatment. However, he described how migrants help one another to cover expensive health care services. When a needed treatment runs into the thousands of dollars, or if someone is out of work and in need of care, relatives, friends, and coworkers pitch in to help cover the costs.

Isabel, a 50-year-old naturalized U.S. citizen currently residing in Arizona, also visiting Tlacuitapa at the time of our fieldwork, reported that costs prohibited her from accessing health care services. While waiting for her public health care benefits to be approved, Isabel was forced to cancel a pending appointment because she could not pay for the service out of pocket. She mentioned that her mother, also an immigrant, could not pay for her glaucoma medications because of the high cost. In the past few months she had already paid $200, and she was unable to have more prescriptions filled because she could not afford them all. Lucia has medical insurance through her husband's employment in Chicago. Despite this, she also spoke of the unaffordable costs of her prescriptions and shared how she is able to obtain them. Instead of buying them in the United States, she has her brother in Tlacuitapa ship her medications to Chicago, lowering her cost for a single prescription from $130 to less than $10.

Discrimination as a Barrier

Though not asked about in our standardized survey, during our qualitative interviews Tlacuitapenses frequently mentioned discrimination a barrier to health care. For example, regarding her most recent hospital visit in Oklahoma, Beatriz said, "I didn't like the service I received. I guess because they see we're Hispanic." In addition to discrimination because of her ethnicity, she also reported discrimination due to documentation status. She reported that health professionals can tell the documented from the undocumented because of the latter's inability to present social security numbers. Beatriz believes that while her U.S. citizen daughters receive quality care, she does not because of her irregular status and her ethnicity. "They [health professionals] know our situation, I think it's racism, discrimination. I don't know how to describe it." When she gets ill she avoids going to any health care facility as much as possible.

DISCUSSION

As expected, we found that among Tlacuitapenses living in the United States the principal challenges to accessing health care services were language barriers, financial barriers, and fear due to undocumented status. We also discovered other barriers, including discrimination, fear of discrimination, fear of language problems, and fear of the high cost of health services. Our findings support our hypothesis that undocumented Tlacuitapenses access fewer health care services than the documented, which is consistent with previous studies by Vargas Bustamante et al. (2012) and Fuentes-Afflick and Hessol (2009). We also discovered that Tlacuitapenses in Oklahoma, regardless of immigration status, have lower rates of accessing health care services, as compared with Tlacuitapenses in California. In addition, fewer Tlacuitapenses in Oklahoma report having a primary care provider than those living in California, which could be due to Oklahoma's attempts at passing restrictive immigration measures in the last decade (García et al., 2011).

Like Quesada et al., (1976) and Andersen et al., (1981), our study found that language continues to be a significant barrier to accessing health care services, especially at hospitals. Several of our Oklahoma interviewees reported that there are no Spanish-speaking staff members at hospitals, and said they avoid hospitals unless they can find someone to accompany them and help translate. Of concern is the high proportion of translations by friends and family who are not trained in medical terminology. Nine percent of translators were minors and it is likely they did not capture everything that was being communicated. It is highly probable that even adults may not be able to translate efficiently in a medical setting. Although Delia was able to get her daughter-in-law to translate for her during a visit to a private physician, she admits that her relative's English abilities are quite limited. It is unknown how much information was missed during that office visit.

Financial barriers kept many Tlacuitapenses from receiving needed medical attention. Numerous interviewees described their inability to pay for office visits, procedures, and treatments. Fear of costs kept many away, especially when they were unaware of how much they might end up owing and feared going into debt. Lucia feared increasing the amount she already owed, while Beatriz feared just being in debt and not knowing how her financial status would affect her immigration status now or in the future.

Discrimination was often mentioned as a reason to avoid seeking health care services when needed. Some believed the discrimination was triggered by the inability to speak English while others believe it was because of their nationality. However, many undocumented migrants recalled noticing a change when their legal status was revealed. A troubling finding is that this discrimination exists even at the hands of Latino medical staff. To some interviewees, discrimination was something they simply wanted to avoid, while others mentioned being afraid of discriminatory treatment.

Fear due immigration status led one in three of our undocumented respondents to avoid seeking care. It is unclear what type of care they needed, or if any of their conditions were transmittable. Fear seemed to be greater when dealing with hospitals than with clinics or private physicians, due to forms and questions hospital staff ask before treatment. Alberto's fear of deportation eventually subsided with time, knowledge, and experience in the United States. By contrast, Beatriz has lived in Oklahoma for ten years and her fear is constant and unrelenting.

Whether living in Oklahoma or some other state, many Tlacuitapenses have developed strategies to cope with perceived barriers to health care. By taking a relative to translate, or pooling money, or finding a safe physician, Tlacuitapenses often get at least the most needed health services. Dr. Tran in Oklahoma City is a physician who helps Tlacuitapenses deal with all of the key barriers to care. He was brought up by many interviewees who have lived in Oklahoma. He was described as affordable, and participants said they go to him in order to avoid expensive hospital bills. Because he knows some Spanish, there is no need to wait to find a translator before going to his clinic. Most importantly, most Tlacuitapenses are aware that he does not ask any questions regarding status and there is no need to fear going to see him. Additionally, Dr. Tran believes many of his patients come to him because they are able to walk in without an appointment. Although many mentioned him, not everyone was aware of him; Delia, for example, did not know about him at the time of our interview. Also, at least one interviewee, Beatriz, was not very satisfied with his Spanish skills and services. Still, she admits that when she does not have a friend to translate for her, she prefers going to Dr. Tran rather than to a hospital.

RECOMMENDATIONS

Cleveland and Ihara (2012), acknowledge that some health care facilities have improved and provide culturally and linguistically appropriate services. Nevertheless, studies continue to demonstrate that some facilities are in need of improvement. Based on our research we can offer several specific recommendations.

At all health care facilities, in order to decrease anxiety and fears, we recommend customer service trainings to prepare staff to treat all patients with respect, regardless of status, language abilities, or ethnicity. We reiterate the recommendation of Hacker et al. (2012) that health care facilities ensure that their environment is perceived as safe, which could be accomplished with posted notifications of patient confidentiality rules. We also recommend that all facilities have affordable payment plans.

Like Cavazos-Rehg et al. (2007), we recommend having bilingual and bicultural staff at health care facilities. Due to the tendency of immigrants to visit hospitals for urgent medical matters, we recommend having on-call translators around the clock at these facilities. For immigrant advocates, we recommend advocating for English-as-a-second-language courses to be made available at no or low cost. Once migrants are empowered to communicate proficiently in English, their fear will subside and their confidence will increase, perhaps to the point they feel capable to seek services at all types of medical facilities. Finally, at the federal policy level, while we support the passage of comprehensive immigration reform, we believe it is not enough to address all the barriers migrants encounter when accessing health care services; truly universal health insurance coverage is urgently needed.

REFERENCES

Andersen, R., Lewis, S.Z., Giachello, A.L., Adday, L.A., and Chiu, G. (1981). Access to Medical Care Among the Hispanic Population of the Southwestern United States. Journal of Health and Social Behavior; 22 (1), 78–89.

Berk, M., and Schur, C. (2001). The Effect of Fear on Access to Care Among Undocumented Latino Immigrants. Journal of Immigrant Health, 3(3), 151–156.

Cavazos-Rehg, P.A., Zayas, L.H., and Spitznagel, E.L. (2007). Legal Status, Emotional Well-being and Subjective Health Status of Latino Immigrants. Journal of the National Medical Association, 99(10),1126–1131.

Cleveland, C., and Ihara, E.S. (2012). 'They Treat Us Like Pests:' Undocumented Immigrant Experiences Obtaining Health Care in the Wake of a 'Crackdown' Ordinance. Journal of Human Behavior in the Social Environment, 22(7), 771–788

Cristancho, S., Garces, D.M., Peters, K.E., and Mueller, B.C. (2008). Listening to Rural Hispanic Immigrants in the Midwest: A Community-Based Participatory Assessment of Major Barriers to Health Care Access and Use. Qualitative Health Research, 18(5), 633–646.

Dang, B.N., Giordano, T.P., and Kim, J.H., (2012). Sociocultural and structural barriers to care among undocumented Latino immigrants with HIV infection. Journal of Immigrant and Minority Health, 14(1), 124-131.

Documét, P.I., and Sharma R.K.. Latinos' Health Care Access: Financial and Cultural Barriers. Journal of Immigrant Health,6(1), 5–13.

Fuentes-Afflick, E., and Hessol, A (2009). Immigration Status and Use of Health Services Among Latina Women in the San Francisco Bay Area. Journal of Women's Health, 18(8), 1275–1280.

Garcia, A., Griesbach, K., Andrade, J., González, C., and Yrizar, G. (2011). Pressure from the inside: The subnational politics of immigration. In In D.S . FitzGerald, R. Alarcon, and L. Muse-Orlinoff (Eds.), Recession Without Borders: Mexican Migrants Confront the Economic Downturn (37-61). La Jolla, CA: Center for Comparative Immigration Studies, UCSD.

Hacker, K., Chu, J., Arsenault, L., and Marlin, R.P. (2012). Provider's Perspectives on the Impact of Immigration and Customs Enforcement (ICE) Activity on Immigrant Health. Journal of Health Care for the Poor and Underserved,23 (2), 651–665.

Hacker, K., Chu, J., Leung, C., Marra, R., Pirie, A., Brahimi, M., English, M., Beckmann, J., Acevedo-García, D., and Marlin R.P.. (2011). The Impact of Immigration and Customs Enforcement on Immigrant Health: Perceptions of Immigrants in Everett, Massachusetts, USA. Social Science & Medicine, 73(4), 586–594.

Heyman, J. M., Nuñez, G.G., and Talavera, V. (2009). Healthcare Access and Barriers for Unauthorized Immigrants in El Paso County, Texas. Family & Community Health, 32(1), 4–21.

Maldonado, C. Z., Rodriguez R.M., Torres J.R., Flores Y.S. and Lovato L.M. (2013). Fear of Discovery Among Latino Immigrants Presenting to the Emergency Department. Academic Emergency Medicine ,20 (2),155–161.

National Immigration Law Center. (2013). Analysis of Immigration Reform Bill Title II: Immigrant Visas. Retrieved from http://www.nilc.org/irsenate2013.html

Oristian, E., Sweeney ,P., Puentes, V., Jimenez, J., Matus, M. (2009). The Migrant Health Paradox Revisited. In: Cornelius, W., FitzGerald D., & Borger, S. (Eds.) (217-239) Four Generations of Norteños: New Research from the Cradle of Mexican Migration. La Jolla, CA: Center for Comparative Immigration Studies, UCSD.

Ortega A.N., Fang, H., Perez V.H., Rizzo J.A., Carter-Pokras, O., Wallace, S.P., and Gelberg, L. (2007). Health Care Access, Use of Services, and Experiences Among Undocumented Mexicans and Other Latinos. Archives of Internal Medicine, 167(21), 2354–2360.

Pew Research Hispanic Center. (2013). A Portrait of the 40 Million, Including 11 Million Unauthorized A Nation of Immigrants. Retrieved from: http://www.pewhispanic.org/2013/01/29/a-nation-of-immigrants

Quesada, Gustavo M. "Language and communication barriers for health delivery to a minority group." Social Science & Medicine (1967) 10.6 (1976): 323-327.

Vargas Bustamante, A., Fang, H., Garza, J., Carter-Pokras, O. Wallace, S.P., Rizzo, J.A., Ortega, A.N. (2012).Variations in Healthcare Access and Utilization Among Mexican Immigrants: The Role of Documentation Status. Journal of Immigrant and Minority Health, 14(1), 146–155.

Wong-Kim, E., Chilton, J.A., Goh S.S., and Gines V. (2013). Breast Health Issues of Undocumented Women in California and Texas. Journal of Cancer Education, 24 (2), S64–S67.

Resumen

Temor y otras barreras en el acceso de los tlacuitapenses a los servicios de salud.

Dinorah L. Sánchez, Catherine Elizabeth Benson,
y Miriam Adriana Arredondo Cervantes

Varios estudios han investigado las barreras a la atención de la salud que afectan a las poblaciones migrantes en los Estados Unidos. Estos estudios han encontrado que el idioma, los costos y el estatus migratorio son causa de que los migrantes retrasen o eviten acudir a servicios de salud. Nuestro estudio, a diferencia de otros anteriores, utilizar métodos cualitativos y cuantitativos para analizar las barreras para la atención a la salud de los migrantes de una comunidad binacional cuyo origen es Tlacuitapa, México.

Se encontró que los tlacuitapenses se enfrentan a barreras en su atención debido a diversas formas de temor, al idioma, a los costos de los servicios y a la percepción de discriminación. Nuestros resultados muestran que los indocumentados tienen menos probabilidades de acceder a los servicios de atención de la salud y más probabilidades de manifestar temor por revelar su estatus migratorio, por ello, disuaden o retrasan la atención.

También mostramos que los migrantes documentados e indocumentados se enfrentan a las barreras del idioma al acceder a servicios de salud, y con frecuencia deben encontrar la forma de acompañarse de sus propios traductores. Independientemente de vivir en Estados Unidos como migrante documentado o indocumentado, los tlacuitapenses reportaron sentir temor por asumir deudas derivadas del uso de servicios de salud, por ser discriminados y por con comprender indicaciones o manifestar necesidades debido al idioma.

Además, hemos encontrado que los tlacuitapenses que viven en California tienen mejor acceso a la atención en salud que quienes residen en Oklahoma. Lo anterior se infirió al conocer cuántas personas tienen un proveedor de atención primaria, y cuántas han acudido a servicios de salud en los últimos 12 meses.

Nuestros resultados indican que todavía hay mucho por hacer para aumentar el acceso a servicios de salud de la población migrante. Conocer las barreras a la atención de la población migrante, ayudará a reducir los obstáculos y a mejorar la salud de una de las poblaciones más vulnerables de Estados Unidos.

Portrait of a Tlacuitapense. (Photograph by Risa Farrell)

4 MANAGEMENT OF CHRONIC DISEASE: DIABETES AND HEALTH SEEKING BEHAVIOR IN A BINATIONAL MIGRANT COMMUNITY

JONATHAN GÓMEZ, GILBERTO LÓPEZ, ALICIA DENISSE VEGA PÉREZ, JESSENIA NÚÑEZ AND BERNARDO LÓPEZ

> *I wasn't well informed about diabetes; I thought it came from inheritance, from family members. Since I didn't have any family with diabetes I did not expect to become diabetic. But the doctor told me that diabetes didn't only come through family history… [but also] diet and obesity.*—Guadalupe, a 26-year-old migrant with diabetes

Guadalupe is a migrant from Tlacuitapa, is in her 20s, and suffers from diabetes. Like many migrants, Guadalupe's life is split between the US and Mexico; living part of the year in Oklahoma City in order to maintain a stable source of income while spending her vacation time in Tlacuitapa visiting those she left behind. Two years ago, while living in Oklahoma, Guadalupe was diagnosed with diabetes during a routine visit to her gynecologist. After being diagnosed she was referred to a specialist, put on medication, referred to a nutritionist, and encouraged to become more physically active. Guadalupe acknowledges that although she was aware of her bad eating habits and her extra weight, she never suspected she was at risk for diabetes. Today Guadalupe is able to maintain control of her illness but wonders how things could be different if she had known how to prevent it. Guadalupe's story is not uncommon among migrants. It highlights several health seeking patterns that influence people's health risks and outcomes.

Despite the growing literature on chronic disease within the various Latino subgroups, especially Mexican immigrants, little has been done in the context of a single binational migrant community (Nandi et al., 2008; Argeseanu, Ruben and Narayan, 2008; Sobralske, 2006). This chapter aims to fill this void by analyzing the social, cultural, and economic factors that influence: interaction dynamics between individuals and their available health systems; nutritional practices; and physical activity, within the context of a single Mexican transnational community. Of special interest is the interplay between the three above-stated factors and diabetes-related health.

In understanding the effects of these intersections, we ask: (a) How do the interaction dynamics between formal health systems and Tlacuitapenses influence diabetes related health? (b) What are the nutritional practices of Tlacuitapenses in this binational community? What is the relationship between nutritional practice and diabetes-related health? (c) What exercise practices are most common within this community, and how do these practices affect diabetes-related health? Understanding the social and environmental factors that influence health can provide a more nuanced understanding of health and illness within migrant communities; information which can in turn be used to design, implement, and evaluate public health interventions aimed at improving health outcomes (Hjelm, Sundquist and Apelquist, 2002; MacKian, 2003).

LITERATURE REVIEW

The burden of chronic disease is an emergent public health priority as evidenced by the increase, in the past twenty years, of literature investigating the burden of non-communicable diseases (NCD) and what has been called lifestyle diseases (Glasgow et al., 1999; Daviglus et al., 2012; WHO, 2003; Sharma and Majumdar, 2009). The emergence of these diseases have been linked to changes in dietary intake and physical activity -- both leading causes of preventable illness in developing and non-developing countries. Changing dietary patterns and physical activity are estimated to be the underlying factors in 60 percent of deaths worldwide (WHO, 2003; Sharma and Majumdar, 2009). Of special concern is the inverse pattern of chronic illness when analyzed globally: it is associated with affluence in developing countries and poverty in industrialized countries

(WHO, 2003). The United States is no exception to this global pattern, as diabetes has reached epidemic proportions in communities of lower socioeconomic status, especially in the Latino community (Robbins et al., 2005; Paeratakul et al., 2002; Connolly et al., 2000; WHO, 2003).

Diabetes is now a major public health priority in the United States, where prevalence tripled between 1990 and 2010 (CDC, 2012). Experts predict that by 2050 one in three Americans will have diabetes (Boyle et al., 2010). The epidemic is especially grim in Latino communities, where diabetes-related deaths make up 4.5 percent of all deaths -- nearly twice that of whites (CDC, 2011). This is especially concerning given that Hispanics are both the largest and fastest growing minority group, estimated to reach one-third of the population by 2050 (Suro 2005, El Nasser 2004; United States Census Bureau Office, 2012a).

The diabetes epidemic is especially prevalent among Mexican-origin and immigrant communities in the United States. Mexico-born persons are the largest national origins group, accounting for 30 percent of foreign-born Americans (United States Census Bureau Office, 2012a). This trend is projected to continue. With one in five U.S. residents being immigrants by 2050, a large proportion of whom will be of Mexican origin (Breslau, 2011). In addition, Mexican-Americans currently have the highest diabetes prevalence of any Latino subgroup, at 19 percent (Daviglus et al., 2012).

Interaction Dynamics with Health Systems

It is understood that the concept of health seeking behavior covers a fairly broad, and well-researched, area that includes individual-focused theories.[1] The analysis in this chapter does not attempt to adhere to any one specific theory. Instead, health seeking behavior is used as a broader concept to include any action, idea, or speech that can influence an individual's risk for diabetes.

One area where analysis of health seeking behaviors can help us in understanding illness is in interaction dynamics with health systems, or the interaction between individuals and their available healthcare system.

---

1. Some of them are Fishbein's Theory of Reasoned Action, Sherif and colleagues Social Judgment Theory, Petty's Elaboration Likelihood Model and Bandura's Social Learning Theory.

The quality of this interaction has been established as an important factor in control of diabetes (Lipton et al., 1998, Zgibor and Songer, 2001; MacKian, 2003). In addition, nutritional intake and level of physical activity are widely acknowledged risk factors for diabetes (Colberg et al., 2010; Hjelm, Sundquist and Apelquist, 2002).

Interactions dynamics with health systems has been used to explain health-seeking behavior in diverse communities (MacKian, 2003). Previously, health seeking behavior has been focused in the practices of individuals, instead of interactions between populations and health systems. Interaction dynamics consists of the collective social element of health seeking behavior; the interaction of individuals and societies with health systems (MacKian, 2003). Management of chronic illness requires close collaboration between clinicians and patients to monitor changes in lifestyle behavior. Interaction dynamics allows for a better understanding of this collaboration (Holman and Lorig, 2000).

Diabetes is a disease with a high health-care burden and increasing prevalence, with one-fourth of those with the disease being undiagnosed (CDC, 2012a). Prolonged lifestyle interventions through nutritional counseling have yielded significant reduction in diabetes incidence. However, access to these and other forms of medical care is sparse in the Latino community, especially among migrants, and is tied to perceived racial discrimination, language differences, and insurance status (Lindström et al., 2011; Dey and Lucas, 2006; Arcury and Quandt, 2007; Solis et al. 1990; Mainous et al., 2006; Marks et al.,1987; Tocher and Larson, 1998). Furthermore, there is a lack of medical knowledge on diabetes among the Mexican-American community, adding to the barriers for care (Coonrod et. al., 1994; Anderson et al., 1998; Lujan et al., 2007). The combination of these factors helps explain the lack of access to preventative care among Mexican immigrants, in turn providing insights into the factors leading to higher incidence of diabetes within this population.

Blood glucose exams, nutritional counseling, and preventative education relies on consistent access to medical care and personnel. Studies show that Latino migrants, when compared to U.S.-born Latinos, are two times less likely to have a constant place of care and three times less likely to have talked with a healthcare professional in their lifetime (Dey and Lucas, 2006). In their study, Phillips, Mayer and Aday (2000) found that Latinos perceive accessing care to be the biggest barrier to health, followed by a lack of needed care, no standard health care source, and longer waits for care.

Language and culture can provide additional barriers to preventive care for diabetes among Mexican migrants. Barriers to communication, linguistic or cultural, are likely to hinder access to preventative diabetes care (Lipton, et al., 1998). In a study on Mexican-Americans, language differences predicted access to preventative services such as routine physical exams and visits with a health professional (Solis et al., 1990). A study by Mainous et al. (2006) found that Hispanics with lower levels of English were less likely to have proper access to health care, including lack of health insurance and no standard health care provider. Studies have also shown improved access to care across language and cultural backgrounds. One study of English- and non-English speaking elderly Hispanic women found that socio-demographic factors such as access to clinical care may be stronger predictors of preventative care than spoken language or acculturation (Marks et al., 1987). Furthermore, a study of non-English speaking patients with type 2 diabetes showed that non-English speaking patients received care that more closely met the ADA recommendations (Tocher and Larson, 1998).

Information about diabetes

Education and informed decision-making are essential components of diabetes prevention, especially for at-risk populations. Lujan et al. (2007), found that culturally relevant health education was positively correlated with decrease in A1C levels among Mexican-Americans. Nonetheless, education and awareness about diabetes is low in Mexican-American and Mexican immigrant communities. Coonard et al. (1994) found that Mexican-Americans had the lowest levels of diabetes education when compared to other ethnic groups. Another study found that social factors such as lack of family support, education, and information contribute to low diabetes awareness and understanding in the community (Anderson et al., 1998).

Access to diabetes preventative services is also influenced by lack of health insurance and its economic implications (Zgibor and Songer, 2001). In the United States 30.7 percent of Hispanics are uninsured, with rates among uninsured migrants being 2.5 times the number of uninsured natives (United States Census Bureau Office Office, 2012b). Lack of insurance has been linked with increased risk of diabetes, via a lack of regular access to preventative care (Ayanian et al., 2000). A study done among diabetic patients reported that up to 49 percent of interviewees did not self monitor sugar levels because of high out of pocket cost. Of special concern for immigrant communities is the restrictive effect of undocumented status on health insurance coverage and health care access (Pérez-Escamilla et al., 2010). One study showed children of Latino farmworkers receive half their medical care in Mexico due to uninsured status and ease of access (Seid et al., 2003).

In this chapter health seeking behavior is analyzed using self-reported data including but not limited to (a) having a diabetes check in the last year, (b) having seen a health professional in the last year, and (c) having a primary health practitioner.

Nutrition and Diabetes

Excessive intake of energy-dense foods with poor satiety value is known to play a significant role in the etiology of chronic disease. Such foods include sugars, which in the United States (and Mexico) are consumed in highly sweetened soft drinks—the leading source of sugars in the population's diet (Ludwig, 2002).

One explanation for a higher calorie intake is the appropriation of U.S. dietary patterns by immigrants (Ulmann et al., 2011). More acculturated Mexican immigrants have higher fat intake and eat 50 percent less servings of fruits and vegetables than do their less acculturated counterparts, as defined by length of residence (Neuhouser et al., 2004). One paradox in the literature on food consumption is that the diet of Mexican immigrants puts them at higher risk of diabetes, while the diets of Mexican non-migrants prove to be protective against diabetes (Jimenez-Cruz et al., 2003).

Physical Activity and Diabetes

Consistent with changes in energy consumption, a decline in energy expenditure is another factor largely implicated in the etiology of chronic disease (Caprio et al., 2008; Ebbeling, Pawlak, and Ludwig, 2002). Physical activity is a widely acknowledged factor involved in both prevention and control of diabetes; moderate intensity exercise increases metabolic control and moderation of blood glucose levels, reducing the risk of type 2 diabetes. (Daviglus et al., 2012). Nowadays however, many adults spend a significant proportion of their time in sedentary pursuits with less time spent on active exercise (Hills, 2009).

Research looking at migration and fitness found that socio-economic barriers, such as immigrant status and poverty, were strong predictors of fitness levels. Not being able to access a place to conduct physical exercise, living in impoverished neighborhoods, and not having U.S. permanent legal residency/citizenship are all factors that predict risk of diabetes among migrants (Perez-Escamilla, 2007). In a study conducted by Mier, Medina and Ory (2007), all participants acknowledged that one of the major barriers to physical activity was not having the time because of work and family obligations. Social barriers to exercise may be a leading factor influencing risk for chronic disease among Mexican immigrants.

TLACUITAPENSES AND DIABETES

Our overall sample consisted of 606 Tlacuitapenses between 18 and 65 years of age, 7 percent of whom had diabetes. Sixty-one percent of interviewees reported a family history of diabetes. Fifty-nine percent were overweight, according to calculated BMI values from self-reported height and weight (BMI ≥ 25) (see table 4.1). The average age of study participants was 37 years.

Table 4.1 BMI by gender

Weight group (BMI)	Male	Female	Overall
Underweight	1.80%	6.55%	4.49%
Normal	31.98%	40.34%	36.72%

Overweight	40.09%	28.97%	33.79%
Obese	16.67%	13.45%	14.84%
Severely obese	5.86%	6.21%	6.05%
Morbidly obese	3.60%	4.48%	4.10%
Total	43.36%	56.64%	512

INTERACTIONAL DYNAMICS BETWEEN INDIVIDUALS AND HEALTH SYSTEMS

Diabetes Testing

In this study, interactional dynamics between individuals and health systems was measured by several variables, the first of which was having had a diabetes test in the last year.[2] To screen for diabetes the American Diabetes Association (ADA) recommends regular testing for all overweight adults (BMI ≥25) who have any of the known risk factors for diabetes, which include physical inactivity, hypertension, high cholesterol, heart disease and first-degree relatives with diabetes (American Diabetes Association, 2013).

Our data showed that 55 percent of immigrants reported a diabetes test in the last year, compared to 53 percent among non-migrants. When including only those who fit the ADA's criteria for at-risk of diabetes, the testing rate was 52 percent, compared to 34 percent for those not at-risk – a statistically significant difference at the 0.001 level. Among migrants 60 percent of those who are documented reported receiving a diabetes test in the last year, while only 46 percent of undocumented migrants reported a test in the last year (p-value = 0.2274).

Gender was another significant determinant of diabetes testing. Females reported testing within the last year at a rate of 64 percent compared to 38 percent among males -- a significant difference at the 0.001 level. When controlling for legal status, 40 percent of documented males, 82 percent of documented females, 42 percent of undocumented males, and 75 percent of

---

2. A diabetes test is defined as any clinical test for diabetes including HbA1C, blood glucose, and oral glucose tests (American Diabetes Association, 2013).

undocumented females had been tested (table 4.2). Using multiple regression models that controlled for wealth, fear, documentation, and education, being male was found to be inversely related to diabetes testing. Males were twice as likely to not have been tested in the past year as females ($p < 0.01$).

Table 4.2 Diabetes testing within recommended group

		Tested	**Untested**
Overall		52.21%	47.79%
	males	37.62%***	62.38%***
	females	64.00%***	36.00%***
Documented		60.29%	39.71%
	males	40.00%**	60%**
	females	81.82%**	18.18%**
Undocumented		45.95%	54.05%
	males	42.42%**	57.58%**
	females	75%**	25%**
Migrant		54.72%	45.28%
Non-migrant		52.63%	47.37%
Income quartile	first	54.05%	45.95%
	second	36.36%	63.64%
	third	45.45%	54.55%
	fourth	58.33%	41.67%
Education quartile	first	50.00%	50.00%
	second	64.71%	35.29%
	third	51.22%	48.78%
	fourth	48.84%	51.16%

Practitioner-patient dynamics

Interaction dynamics with health systems was also measured through the number of visits with a health practitioner in the last twelve months. Disease prevention requires collaborative partnerships between provider and patient in order to modify and maintain reductions in behavioral risk (American

Diabetes Association, 2013; WHO, 2003; Holman and Lorig, 2000). One important factor in the success of these partnerships is consistent check-ups and follow-ups with a health practitioner (American Diabetes Association, 2013). Our data show that 60 percent of interviewees reported visiting a health practitioner at least once in the last twelve months, with a median number of visits of 2. Further statistical analysis showed that gender and education were significant predictors of visiting a provider in the last twelve months. Males reported visiting a practitioner at a rate of 48 percent, compared to 68 percent of females ($p < 0.001$).

Analysis of documentation and gender showed that 51 percent of documented males, 71 percent of documented females, 47 percent of undocumented males, and 71percent of undocumented females reported a visit in the last 12 months ($p = 0.008$). In analyzing education, the data were divided into quartiles, which revealed a significant relationship with testing (see table 4.3).

Table 4.3 Practitioner visits (last 12 months)

		Yes	No
Overall		60.00%	40.00%
	males	47.74%***	52.26%***
	females	68.33%***	31.67%***
Documented		60.00%	40.00%
	males	50.75%**	49.25%**
	females	70.69%**	29.31%**
Undocumented		52.99%	47.01%
	males	46.51%**	53.49%**
	females	70.97%**	29.03%**
Migrants		56.73%	43.27%
Non-migrants		70.91%	29.09%

Primary care

Another important factor in managing lifestyle disease is ensuring access to preventative health and primary care services (WHO, 2003). In our survey 51 percent of migrant respondents reported having a primary care provider (PCP). When analyzed by gender, data showed a significant difference in PCP between genders with 42 percent of males and 64 percent of females having a PCP (p < 0.001). Analysis of legal status and gender found significant relationships between the two variables and having a PCP with 61 percent of documented males, 66 percent of documented females, 25 percent of undocumented males, and 78 percent of undocumented females having a PCP (p < 0.001). In the United States, documentation status was also found to be a statistically significant predictor of having a PCP. Sixty-three percent of documented migrants reported having a PCP, compared to 37 percent of undocumented migrants (p < 0.001). Among those living in the United States, 22.8 percent reported problems understanding their doctor due to language issues (see table 4.4).

Table 4.4 Primary care practitioner

		Yes	No
Overall		51.34%	48.66%
	males	42.26%***	57.74%***
	females	63.55%***	36.45%***
Documented		63.41%***	36.59%***
	males	61.19%***	38.81%***
	females	66.07%***	33.93%***
Undocumented		37.37%***	62.63%***
	males	25.00%***	75.00%***
	females	78.26%***	21.74%***

Information

One of the questions asked in our survey was "Have you ever received information about diabetes?" We found that 39 percent of respondents reported having received information about diabetes, while 61 percent reported never having received any information. Digging deeper into these data, several factors were controlled in order to further understand the relationships between educational information and diabetes (see table 4.5).

When accounting for place of residence, the data showed that 42 percent of those living in the United States have received some sort of educational information about diabetes, while only 38 percent of those residing in Mexico had received information. Income was divided into quartiles and analyzed for having received information about diabetes. Differences in education and diabetes information received were statistically significant. Legal immigration status was another important determinant of diabetes education. Forty-three percent of documented immigrants reported receiving information about diabetes, compared to just 22 percent of those without documents (p-value = 0.001). Men were significantly, at the 0.001 level, less likely to report having received information about diabetes than females. Among those who received information about diabetes only 3.1 percent reported not receiving it in their preferred language.

Table 4.5 Information about diabetes

	Sub-group	Yes	No
Gender	Male	30.20%	69.80%
	Female	45.15%	54.85%
Migratory Experience	Migrant	32.52%	67.48%
	Non-migrant	50.00%	50.00%
Legal Status in US	Documented	42.86%	57.15%
	Undocumented	22.22%	77.88%
Education (years)	0-6	27.72%	72.58%
	6-8	37.21%	62.79%
	8-11	41.23%	58.77%
	11-36	50.44%	49.56%

Nutrition

Analysis by gender showed significant differences in four food types, with females consuming more of the foods considered protective by prevention specialists. Females consumed fruits at a rate of 21 percent while their male counterparts showed a consumption rate of 13 percent, a significant difference at the 0.05 level. Women also consumed significantly more dairy products (43 percent) than men (28 percent). Men consumed both seafood and alcohol at rates significantly different than females. Seafood was consumed by males at a rate of 13 percent, compared to 7 percent among females. Alcohol was the food with the biggest significance, with 16 percent of males reporting drinking, compared to less than one percent of females (figure 4.1).

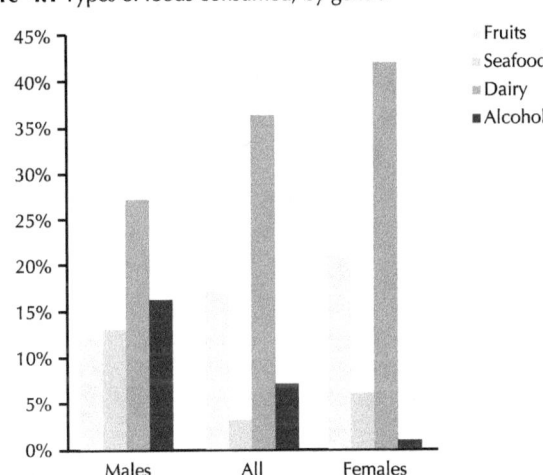

Figure 4.1 Types of foods consumed, by gender

Analysis by geographic location showed that interviewees living in the United States were more like to eat red meat, wheat/flour, seafood, dark green vegetables (broccoli, lettuce, spinach), and to eat nothing (skip a meal). Individuals currently living in Mexico are more likely to eat non-fried legumes (beans, lentils, chickpeas), fried foods (beans, potatoes, chicken, vegetables), pasta (spaghetti, noodles, etc.), eggs, and tortillas.

Sixty percent of respondents living in the United States reported consuming red meat, compared to 46 percent of those living in Mexico (p-value 0.004). Flour or wheat foods were consumed at a rate of 38 percent among those living in the United States compared to 19 percent among those currently living in Mexico. Seafood consumption was also significantly different, with those living in the United States consuming at a rate of 16 percent and those living in Mexico at just 7 percent. Twenty-six percent of respondents living in the United States reported the consumption of dark green vegetables (broccoli, lettuce, spinach) while 15 percent of those living in Mexico reported eating dark green vegetables. Skipping a meal was significantly different between those living in the United States (37 percent) and those living in Mexico (28 percent).

Mexico-based interviewees were significantly more likely to consume certain foods than their U.S. counterparts. Twenty-two percent reported consuming non-fried legumes (beans, lentils, chickpeas) compared to 10 percent of those living in the United States. Forty-two percent of those living in Mexico reported eating fried foods (beans, potatoes, chicken, vegetables), while 19 percent of respondents who live in the United States reported eating fried foods. Pasta was consumed at significantly higher rate among those living in Mexico (10 percent) than among those living in the United States (4 percent). Eggs and tortillas were both foods consumed at significantly higher rates among those living in Mexico, with rates of 29 percent and 60 percent, respectively. In contrast, those living in the United States consumed Eggs and tortillas at rates of 14 percent and 42 percent, respectively (table 4.6).

Table 4.6. Types of food consumed, by place of residence

Food consumed	Mexico	USA	P-value
Red meat	46.4	59.8	0.004
Wheat/flours	18.7	38.3	< 0.001
No meal	28.3	37.1	0.047
Legumes	22.5	9.6	< 0.001
Seafood	6.8	16.2	0.001
Fried food	42.2	18.6	< 0.001
Pasta	9.8	4.2	0.037

Eggs	28.8	13.8	< 0.001
Green vegetables	15.2	25.8	0.004
Tortillas	59.7	41.9	< 0.001
Red meat	46.4	59.8	0.004
Wheat/flours	18.7	38.3	< 0.001
No meal	28.3	37.1	0.047

When analyzing the relationship between documentation status and nutritional intake, those with legal status consume significantly more non-fried legumes (beans, lentils, chickpeas), eggs and tortillas than undocumented immigrants. Our data shows that those in the country without proper documentation significantly eat more Grain (rice, flaxseed, oats, cereal) than those in the country with documents. Twenty-five percent of the documented said they consumed legumes, compared to 13 percent among the undocumented. Thirty-two percent of documented immigrants reported eating eggs while 17 percent of the undocumented reported the same. Tortillas were consumed at significantly higher rates among the documented (61 percent) than among the undocumented (45 percent) (figure 4.2).

Figure 4.2 Type of food consumed, by immigration status

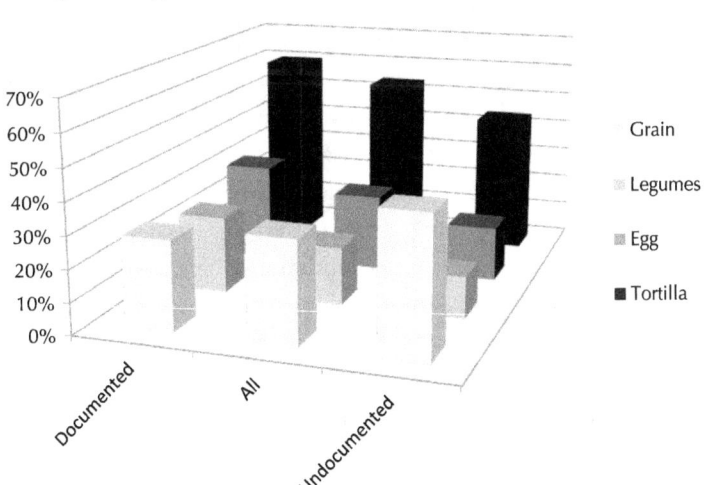

In analyzing the relationship between access to nutrition information and nutrition intake, those who receive information are more likely to consume fruits (23 percent) than those who did not (14 percent). Vegetables were also consumed at significantly different rates between those who had been given nutrition information (43 percent) and those lacking such information (33 percent). Those who did not receive nutritional information consumed significantly less dairy products (33 percent) than those who receive nutritional information (43 percent).

In looking at nutritional patterns, we found that factors including gender, legal status, place of residence, and nutrition information were significant determinants of diets within this community. Of these factors, place of residence proved to be the most influential, accounting for ten statistically significant differences in the type of foods eaten. Understanding why and how such differences are manifested is the next step in understanding nutrition and diabetes within this community.

Physical Activity

To measure physical activity levels, respondents were asked a series of recall questions about the type of activity they had engaged in during the past week, with follow-up questions about the frequency and duration of each selected activity. The activities included working in construction, agricultural work, house cleaning, sports, and walking. Survey data were analyzed using descriptive statistics, cross-tabulations, and multivariate regressions. In addition to survey data, open-ended interviews were conducted with the aim of understanding how, when, or where individuals engage in physical activities as well as how they conceptualize physical activity.

The data reveal that 89.5 percent of respondents reported some form of physical activity in the last week. When analyzed by gender, amount of physical activity became statistically significant in three categories; running, all exercise, and occupational-related physical activity. Males averaged 335 minutes of total physical activity while women averaged 192 minutes. When controlling for additional variables, men averaged 186 more minutes per day of total exercise than women, a statistically significant difference at the 0.001 level. In addition, men averaged 165 more minutes per day of occupational-related physical activity than women, with a p-value of at least 0.001. A third activity where gender differences were significantly different was jogging. Men averaged 57 more minutes of jogging every day than their female counterparts, with significance at the 0.05 level. Age was found to be statistically correlated with four activities: farm work, walking for exercise, all exercise, and occupational-related physical activity. Data show that older individuals dedicate less time to physically demanding activities than do younger individuals. For each additional year of age, individuals conducted farm work on average 9 fewer minutes per day.

With every additional year of age, individuals walked on average 6 fewer minutes per day. When analyzing physical activity as an aggregate it was found that the older someone was, the less time they spent on overall physical activity. For each additional year of age, individuals performed 6 fewer minutes of overall exercise. This pattern also applied to occupational-related physical activity, with individuals participating 5 fewer minutes per day for every additional year of age. When analyzed by age group, those below forty averaged 228 minutes per day of physical activity, compared with 263 for those over forty. Chi-square analysis showed that age and physical activity were dependent on one another. What was interesting was the difference between actual and expected number of individuals conducting occupational-related physical activity, with those above 40 being overrepresented.

When analyzed with other variables, education was not found to have any significant relationships. However, when analyzed independently, Chi-square test showed there was a dependent relation between level of education and type of physical activity. Averages for amount of physical activity by education level were calculated, with education being divided into three categories (elementary, middle, and high). Those with an elementary school education averaged 315 minutes of exercise, those with middle school averaged 238, and high school-educated respondents averaged 199 minutes. A pattern that was observed, but not statistically tested, was that mean occupational-related physical activity was inversely related to educational attainment. Those with a high-school education averaged fewer minutes of occupational-related physical activity than those with an elementary level education. In contrast, individuals with a high school education averaged more time in non-occupational physical activity than those with elementary education.

Migrants averaged 280 minutes of overall physical activity while their non-migrant counterparts averaged 231 minutes. When controlling for additional variables, the data show that migrants performed more physical activities overall than non-migrants and spent more time in occupational-related physical activity than non-migrants. Migrants averaged 125 minutes more per day of overall physical exercise than non-migrants; and 124 minutes more in occupational-related physical activity.

Another surprising finding was the relationship between wealth and jogging for exercise, with data showing an inverse relationship between wealth and jogging. Thus, the wealthier an individual, the less jogging they did.

DISCUSSION

It is well known that diabetes is a serious public health problem among Mexicans and Mexican-Americans (Martorell, 2005). This worrisome fact is reflected in our binational study population, in which 61 percent of Tlacuitapenses reported having a family history of diabetes while 59 percent were overweight themselves. Nonetheless, results showed a surprisingly low 7 percent prevalence of diabetes in the population. This probably reflects the study design, in which only individuals between ages 18 and 65 were interviewed. Epidemiological data have shown that those over age 65 have a diabetes prevalence seven times that of those between the ages of 25 and 44 (CDC, 2011).

Interactions with health systems in order to prevent and manage diabetes were found to be limited, especially among males. Overall testing rates were 52 percent, reaching values as low as 40 percent among documented males. Annual practitioner visits were 50 percent, 47 percent among undocumented males. Only half of our respondents had a primary care practitioner; even more concerning, only one in four undocumented males had a primary care practitioner. Possible reasons for this lack of interaction with the U.S. health care system include fear of deportation, fear of discrimination, and cultural differences (Ryan, Gee, and Griffith, 2008).

Miguel, a migrant, described his experience waiting for medicine for two hours at a clinic: "The doctor said in English, 'he wants medicine?' and they started laughing." As bicultural individuals, migrants face unparalleled barriers to understanding, interpreting, and collaborating with U.S. health providers, who may not attend to, may undervalue, or may misinterpret their values and beliefs about health and illness (Brondino et al., 1997; Brach and Fraserirector, 2000; Holland, 1998).

While characteristic of the overall study population, poor interactions with health systems were a hallmark of the male population, across all measures. Males were significantly ($p < 0.001$) less likely to report diabetes testing, less likely ($p < 0.001$) to have visited a health practitioner in the last 12 months, and less likely to have a primary care physician ($p < 0.001$).

Literature points to socialization and gender roles as factors that play a role in health-seeking behavior among Mexican men. Men are viewed as the sole providers for the family unit, from which they derive a particular social role: the ability to work, support, and provide for their families. As a result, any acknowledgement of pain or illness can be seen as a sign of weakness, a threat to one's masculinity, and ultimate loss of identity (Sobralske, 2006).

Our results further demonstrated the influence of education and documentation on interaction with health systems. Less educated respondents were significantly less likely to visit health care practitioners ($p < 0.05$). A large majority of undocumented migrants did not have a primary care practitioner, suggesting poor system dynamics among this group ($p < 0.001$). Education improves social status and self-efficacy, enabling individuals to "work with the system" to improve health outcomes (Deaton, 2002). Undocumented migrants are particularly vulnerable. Because they are not authorized to work in the United States, exploitation by employers is common.

Maritza, a U.S. citizen and daughter of a migrant, talked about the lack of self-confidence among Mexicans to demand health care in the United States: "Americans always insist on their rights, and we immigrants just hope, because we don't have an alternative." This suggests that improved education and rising social status could be factors in improving interaction with health systems among Tlacuitapenses.

Only 39 percent of the study population reported having received some sort of education about diabetes. When controlling for gender, men were significantly less likely to report having received information about diabetes. Only one in three reported ever having received information about diabetes. This is an alarming result, because Mexican and Mexican-American men have higher rates of diabetes prevalence than non-Hispanic whites and blacks (Martorell, 2005).

U.S. migration experience, legal status, and education were also statistically significant in an individual having received information about diabetes. Only three out of ten migrants reported having received information about diabetes, compared to five of every ten non-migrants. Among those who had migrated to the United States, documentation status also played a role in education about diabetes. Only about two of every ten undocumented migrants reported having received information about diabetes, compared to four out of ten documented migrants.

Such data run counter to the statement of a local doctor in Tlacuitapa, who told us that patients who have been diagnosed with diabetes and have migrated to the United States have greater access to information, medications, and treatment. Our data show this is not the case.

Information is a key form of preventative healthcare in the fight against chronic diseases. Our interviewees in the lowest income and education quartiles were the most likely to not receive information about diabetes, as were undocumented migrants in the United States. This suggests that barriers to diabetes education are highest in the population that has the highest prevalence of diabetes and diabetic complications (Robbins et al., 2005; Paeratakul et al., 2002; Connolly et al., 2000). Lack of information is likely to discourage seeking preventative care and changing nutrition and exercise habits in order to prevent the disease.

CONCLUSION

Our results show intersections of vulnerability resulting in poor health-seeking behavior among undocumented male migrants. Previous studies have shown increased sedentism and poor nutritional intake among migrants (Mier, Medina and Ory, 2007; Perez-Escamilla Putnik, 2007;

Ulmann et al., 2011; Neuhouser et al., 2004 Fitzgerald et al. 2007; Jimenez-Cruz et al., 2003), however these patterns were not obvious from our results. Possible explanations could be unique to the migrant community we were studying, a community with a long-standing migration history and accumulation of social capital in the United States

Our main finding was that male Tlacuitapenses are extremely isolated from the health care system. We ascribe this to Mexican male culture and socialization, which create numerous barriers to care in a westernized health-system that is not competently treating this population (Sobralske, 2006; Brondino et al., 1997; Brach and Fraserirector, 2000). Masculine identity is defined by the male's social role as the sole provider, worker, and backbone of the Mexican family, where any signs of illness or infirmity are seen as a threat to his very identity and a sign of weakness (MacNaughton et al., 2008; Sobralske, 2006). This leads to delayed or non-seeking of care, which is known to lead to worse health-outcomes, especially in terms of chronic disease which requires consistent follow-up and collaboration with a health practitioner (Sobralske, 2006; Holman and Lorig, 2000; WHO, 2003). Future interventions to address this issue include culturally-competent approaches to health care, in order to bridge barriers between the Latino, particularly the Latino male, community and the health-care system.

Culturally competent medicine has been described as an essential component in the elimination of health disparities (Brondino et al., 1997). Men of color are less likely to seek health services. And regardless of income and insurance status, they receive less care and lower quality care (MacNaughton et al., 2008). These are all marks of a culturally incompetent health system that fosters mistrust, misunderstanding, and a lack of confidence in health care providers (Brondino et al., 1997). There is a dearth of research evaluating the effectiveness of interventions to increase cultural competency and improve health outcomes (Brach and Fraserirector, 2000).

Suggestions for improvement include culturally competent health promotions that address the cultural values and perspectives of Mexican and Mexican-American communities. Examples include collaboration with women as "health-care brokers" and interventions using promotoras or lay health advisors (LHAs) (Brach and Fraserirector, 2000; Rhodes et al., 2007). Research shows that women and spouses are often the most influential factor, supporting and encouraging Mexican males to seek medical care (Norcross et al., 1996; Sobralske et al., 2006). Approaches that acknowledge a more family-centric culture may use family to influence health behavior (Schiavenato, 1997). Finally, interventions that incorporate members of the community as gate keepers into the health system show promise in the field (Rhodes et al., 2007; Brach and Fraserirector, 2000). LHAs advocate for migrant men and serve as educators, while connecting them with health services. Undocumented migrant José summarized the factors that played into his lack of care in the United States: "It was due to fear of being deported or rejected for being Mexican." This is a mindset that must be changed in order to achieve health equity in the Mexican immigrant community.

REFERENCES

American Diabetes Association. (2013). Standards of Medical Care in Diabetes--2013. Diabetes Care, 36 (Supplement_1), S11–S66. doi:10.2337/dc13-S011

Ayanian, J. Z., Weissman, J. S., Schneider, E. C., Ginsburg, J. A., & Zaslavsky, A. M. (2000). Unmet health needs of uninsured adults in the United States. JAMA: the journal of the American Medical Association, 284(16), 2061–2069.

Anderson, R. M., Goddard, C. E., Garcia, R., Guzman, J. R., & Vazquez, F. (1998). Using Focus Groups to Identify Diabetes Care and Education Issues for Latinos With Diabetes. The Diabetes Educator, 24(5), 618–624. doi:10.1177/014572179802400507

Argeseanu S., Ruben, J. D., & Narayan, K. M. V. (2008). Health of foreign-born people in the United States: a review. Health & place, 14(4), 623–635. doi:10.1016/j.healthplace.2007.12.002

Arcury, T. A., & Quandt, S. A. (2007). Delivery of Health Services to Migrant and Seasonal Farmworkers. Annual Review of Public Health, 28(1), 345–363. doi:10.1146/annurev.publhealth.27.021405.102106

Boyle, J. P., Thompson, T. J., Gregg, E. W., Barker, L. E., and Williamson, D. F. (2010). Projection of the year 2050 burden of diabetes in the US adult population: dynamic modeling of incidence, mortality, and prediabetes prevalence. Population Health Metrics, 8(1), 29. doi:10.1186/1478-7954-8-29

Brach, C., & Fraserirector, I. (2000). Can Cultural Competency Reduce Racial and Ethnic Health Disparities? a Review and Conceptual Model. Medical Care Research and Review, 57(4 suppl), 181–217. doi:10.1177/1077558700574009

Breslau J, B. G. (2011). Migration from Mexico to the United States and subsequent risk for depressive and anxiety disorders: A cross-national study. Archives of General Psychiatry, 68(4), 428–433. doi:10.1001/archgenpsychiatry.2011.21

Brondino, M. J., Henggeler, S. W., Rowland, M. D., Pickrel, S. G., Cunningham, P. B., & Schoenwald, S. K. (1997). Multisystematic therapy and the ethnic minority client: Culturally responsive and clinically effective. In D. K. Wilson, J. R. Rodrigue, & W. C. Taylor (eds.), Health-promoting and health-compromising behaviors among minority adolescents (pp. 229–250). Washington, DC: American Psychological Association.

Caprio, S., Daniels, S., Drewnowski, A., Kaufman, F.R., Palinkas, L.A., Rosenbloom, A.L., & Schwimmer, J.B. (2008). Influence of Race, Ethnicity, and Culture on Childhood Obesity: Implications for Prevention and Treatment. A consensus statement from Shaping America's Health and the Obesity Society. Diabetes Care 31(11): 2211–2221.

CDC -Centers for Disease Control and Prevention- (2011). National diabetes fact sheet: national estimates and general information on diabetes and prediabetes in the United States, 2011. Atlanta, GA: U.S. Department of Health and Human Services, Centers for Disease Control and Prevention.

CDC -Centers for Disease Control and Prevention-. (2012). Diabetes Report Card 2012.. Atlanta, GA: Centers for Disease Control and Prevention, US Department of Health and Human Services; 2012.

Colberg, S. R., Sigal, R. J., Fernhall, B., Regensteiner, J. G., Blissmer, B. J., Rubin, R. R., Chasan-Taber, L., Albright, A. L., Braun, B. (2010). Exercise and Type 2 Diabetes. Diabetes Care, 33(12), e147–e167. doi:10.2337/dc10-9990

Connolly, V., Unwin, N., Sherriff, P., Bilous, R., & Kelly, W. (2000). Diabetes prevalence and socioeconomic status: a population based study showing increased prevalence of type 2 diabetes mellitus in deprived areas. Journal of Epidemiology and Community Health, 54(3), 173–177.doi:10.1136/jech.54.3.173

Coonrod, B. A., Betschart, J., & Harris, M. I. (1994). Frequency and Determinants of Diabetes Patient Education Among Adults in the U.S. Population. Diabetes Care, 17(8), 852–858.

Daviglus, M. L., Talavera, G. A., Avilés-Santa, M. L., Allison, M., Cai, J., Criqui, M. H., Gellman, M., Giachello, A.L., Gouskova, N., Kaplan, R.C., LaVange, L., Penedo, F., Perreira, K., Pirzada, A., Schneiderman, N., Wassertheil-Smoller, S., Sorlie, P.D., Stamler, J. (2012). Prevalence of major cardiovascular risk factors and cardiovascular diseases among Hispanic/Latino individuals of diverse backgrounds in the United States. Journal of the American Medical Association, 308(17), 1775–1784. doi:10.1001/jama.2012.14517

Deaton, A. (2002). Policy Implications of The Gradient of Health And Wealth. Health Affairs, 21(2), 13–30.

Dey, A. N., & Lucas, J. W. (2006). Physical and mental health characteristics of U.S.- and foreign-born adults: United States, 1998-2003. Advance data, (369), 1–19.

Ebbeling, C.B., Pawlak, D.B., & Ludwig, D.S. (2002) Childhood Obesity: Public-Health Crisis, Common Sense Cure. The Lancet, 360(9331), 473-482

El Nasser, H. (2004). Census Projects Growing Diversity By 2050: Population Burst, Societal Shifts. USA Today. March 18.

Glasgow, R. E., Wagner E.H., Vinicor F., Smith L., and Norman (1999). If diabetes is a public health problem, why not treat it as one? A population-based approach to chronic illness. Annals of Behavioral Medicine, 21(2), 159–170. doi:10.1007/BF02908297

Hills, A.P. (2009). It's Time to Be More Serious about Activating Youngsters: Lessons for Childhood Obesity; Journal of Exercise Science and Fitness (supplement), 7(2), S28-S33.

Hjelm, K., Sundquist, J., & Apelquist, J. (2002). The influence of socio-economic status and life style on self-reported health in diabetics and non-diabetics: a comparison of foreign-born and Swedish-born individuals. Primary Health Care Research & Development, 3(04), 249–259. doi:10.1191/1463423602pc108oa

Holland, L. (1998). Increasing Cultural Competence With the Latino Community. Journal of Community Health Nursing, 15(1), 45–53. doi:10.1207/s15327655jchn1501_5

Holman, H., & Lorig, K. (2000). Patients as partners in managing chronic disease. British Medical Journal, 320(7234), 526–527.

Jimenez-Cruz, A., Bacardi-Gascon, M., Turnbull, W. H., Rosales-Garay, P., & Severino-Lugo, I. (2003). A Flexible, Low-Glycemic Index Mexican-Style Diet in Overweight and Obese Subjects With Type 2 Diabetes Improves Metabolic Parameters During a 6-Week Treatment Period. Diabetes Care, 26(7), 1967–1970. doi:10.2337/diacare.26.7.1967

Lindström, J., Ilanne-Parikka, P., Peltonen, M., Aunola, S., Eriksson, J. G., Hemiö, K., Hämäläinen, H., Härkönen, P., Keinänen-Kiukaanniemi, S., Laakso, M., Louheranta, A., Mannelin, M., Paturi, M., Sundvall, J, Valle, T.T., Uusitupa, M., Tuomilehto, J., Finnish Diabetes Prevention Study Group.(2011). Sustained reduction in the incidence of type 2 diabetes by lifestyle intervention: follow-up of the Finnish Diabetes Prevention Study. The Lancet, 368(9548), 1673–1679. doi:10.1016/S0140-6736(06)69701-8

Lipton, R. B., Losey, L. M., Giachello, A., Mendez, J., & Girotti, M. H. (1998). Attitudes and Issues in Treating Latino Patients With Type 2 Diabetes: Views of Healthcare Providers. The Diabetes Educator, 24(1), 67–71. doi:10.1177/014572179802400109

Ludwig, D. S. (2002). The Glycemic Index: Physiological Mechanisms Relating to Obesity, Diabetes, and Cardiovascular Disease. Journal of the American Medical Association, 287(18), 2414–2423. doi:10.1001/jama.287.18.2414

Lujan, J., Ostwald, S. K., & Ortiz, M. (2007). Promotora diabetes intervention for Mexican Americans. The Diabetes educator, 33(4), 660–670. doi:10.1177/0145721707304080

Klein, S., Sheard, N.F., Pi-Sunyer, X., Daly, A., Wylie-Rosett, J., Kulkarni, K., & Clark, N.G. (2004). Weight Management Through Lifestyle Modification for the Prevention and Management of Type 2 Diabetes: Rationale and Strategies A statement of the American Diabetes Association, the North American Association for the Study of Obesity, and the American Society for Clinical Nutrition. Diabetes Care, 27(8), 2067–2073. doi:10.2337/diacare.27.8.2067

MacKian, S. (2003). A review of health seeking behaviour: problems and prospects. HSD/WP/05/03. Manchester: University of Manchester Health Systems Development Programme.

Mainous, A. G., Majeed, A., Koopman, R. J., Baker, R., Everett, C. J., Tilley, B. C., & Diaz, V. A. (2006). Acculturation and Diabetes Among Hispanics: Evidence from the 1999–2002 National Health and Nutrition Examination Survey. Public Health Reports, 121(1), 60–66.

Marks, G., Solis, J., Richardson, J. L., Collins, L. M., Birba, L., & Hisserich, J. C. (1987). Health behavior of elderly Hispanic women: does cultural assimilation make a difference? American Journal of Public Health, 77(10), 1315–1319.

Martorell, R. (2005). Diabetes and Mexicans: Why the Two Are Linked. Preventing chronic disease [electronic resource]., 2(1). Retrieved fromhttp://www.ncbi.nlm.nih.gov/pmc/articles/PMC1323307/

Mier, N., Medina, A. A., & Ory, M. G. (2007). Mexican Americans With Type 2 Diabetes: Perspectives on Definitions, Motivators, and Programs of Physical Activity. Preventing Chronic Disease, 4(2). Retrieved from http://www.ncbi.nlm.nih.gov/pmc/articles/PMC1893123/

Nandi, A., Galea, S., Lopez, G., Nandi, V., Strongarone, S., & Ompad, D. C. (2008). Access to and Use of Health Services Among Undocumented Mexican Immigrants in a U.S. Urban Area. American Journal of Public Health, 98(11), 2011–2020. doi:10.2105/AJPH.2006.096222

Neuhouser, M. L., Thompson, B., Coronado, G. D., & Solomon, C. C. (2004). Higher fat intake and lower fruit and vegetables intakes are associated with greater acculturation among Mexicans living in Washington State. Journal of the American Dietetic Association, 104(1), 51–57. doi:10.1016/j.jada.2003.10.015

Paeratakul, S., Lovejoy, J. C., Ryan, D. H., & Bray, G. A. (2002). The relation of gender, race and socioeconomic status to obesity and obesity comorbidities in a sample of US adults.International Journal of Obesity and Related Metabolic Disorders, 26(9), 1205–1210. doi:10.1038/sj.ijo.0802026

Pérez-Escamilla, R., Garcia, J., & Song, D. (2010). Health Care Access among Hispanic Immigrants: ¿Alguien está escuchando? [is anybody listening?]. NAPA bulletin, 34(1), 47–67.

Phillips, K. A., Mayer, M. L., & Aday, L. A. (2000). Barriers to care among racial/ethnic groups under managed care. Health Affairs, 19(4), 65–75.doi:10.1377/hlthaff.19.4.65

Rhodes, S. D., Foley, K. L., Zometa, C. S., & Bloom, F. R. (2007). Lay Health Advisor Interventions Among Hispanics/Latinos: A Qualitative Systematic Review. American Journal of Preventive Medicine, 33(5), 418–427. doi:10.1016/j.amepre.2007.07.023

Robbins, J. M., Vaccarino, V., Zhang, H., & Kasl, S. V. (2005). Socioeconomic status and diagnosed diabetes incidence. Diabetes research and clinical practice, 68(3), 230–236. doi:10.1016/j.diabres.2004.09.007

Ryan, A. M., Gee, G. C., & Griffith, D. (2008). The effects of perceived discrimination on diabetes management. Journal of health care for the poor and underserved, 19(1), 149–163. doi:10.1353/hpu.2008.0005

Seid, M., Castañeda, D., Mize, R., Zivkovic, M., & Varni, J. W. (2003). Crossing the border for health care: access and primary care characteristics for young children of Latino farm workers along the US-Mexico border. Ambulatory pediatrics: the official journal of the Ambulatory Pediatric Association, 3(3), 121–130.

Sharma, M., and Majumdar, P. K. (2009). Occupational lifestyle diseases: An emerging issue. Indian Journal of Occupational and Environmental Medicine, 13(3), 109–112. doi:10.4103/0019-5278.58912

Sobralske, M. C. (2006). Health Care Seeking Among Mexican American Men. Journal of Transcultural Nursing, 17(2), 129–138. doi:10.1177/1043659606286767

Solis, J. M., Marks, G., Garcia, M., & Shelton, D. (1990). Acculturation, access to care, and use of preventive services by Hispanics: findings from HHANES 1982-84. American Journal of Public Health, 80 Suppl, 11–19.

Suro, R. (2005). Special Section: Hispanic Americans-A growing Minority. The World   Almanac and Book of Facts 2005. (pp. 7-11) World Almanac Education Group, Inc. New   York, NY.

Tocher, T. M., & Larson, E. (1998). Quality of diabetes care for non-English-speaking patients. A comparative study. Western Journal of Medicine, 168(6), 504–511.

United States Census Bureau Office. (2012a). U.S. Census Bureau Projections Show a Slower Growing, Older, More Diverse Nation a Half Century from Now [Population Release File]. Retrieved from https://www.census.gov/newsroom/releases/archives/population/cb12-243.html

United States Census Bureau Office. (2012b). Income, Poverty and Health Insurance Coverage in the United States: 2011[Poverty Release File]. Retrieved from http://www.census.gov/hhes/www/poverty/data/incpovhlth/2011/

WHO (World Health Organization). (2003). Diet, nutrition, and the prevention of chronic diseases report of a joint WHO/FAO expert consultation. Geneva: World Health Organization.

Zgibor, J. C., & Songer, T. J. (2001). External Barriers to Diabetes Care: Addressing Personal and Health Systems Issues. Diabetes Spectrum, 14(1), 23–28.doi:10.2337/diaspect.14.1.23

Resumen

Manejo de la enfermedad crónica: diabetes y la búsqueda de atención en una comunidad binacional de migrantes

Jonathan Gómez, Gilberto López, Alicia Denisse Vega Pérez, Jessenia Núñez y Bernardo López

La diabetes es considerada una epidemia entre las comunidades migrantes de origen mexicano en los Estados Unidos, ya que estos y sus descendientes forman un 19 por ciento de los diabéticos entre la comunidad Latina.

Este capítulo intenta analizar los factores sociales, culturales y económicos que influyen en la dinámica de interacción entre individuos y los sistemas de salud, así como las practicas de nutrición, actividad física, manteniendo un enfoque en la problemática de la diabetes tipo 2 entre la comunidad binacional tlacuitapense. De especial interés es la interacción entre los tres factores arriba mencionados y la salud relacionados con la diabetes.

En la comprensión de los efectos de estas intersecciones, nos preguntamos: (a) ¿De qué manera la dinámica de interacción entre los sistemas formales de salud y los tlacuitapenses influyen en la salud relacionados con la diabetes? (b) ¿Cuáles son las prácticas nutricionales de los tlacuitapenses en esta comunidad binacional? ¿Cuál es la relación entre la práctica nutricional y la salud relacionados con la diabetes? y (c) ¿Qué prácticas de ejercicio son más comunes dentro de esta comunidad? ¿Cómo estas prácticas afectan a la salud relacionada con la diabetes?

La comprensión de los factores sociales y ambientales que influyen en la salud pueden proporcionar una mejor comprensión de la salud y la enfermedad en las comunidades de migrantes, información que a su vez puede ser utilizado para diseñar, implementar y evaluar intervenciones de salud pública dirigidas a mejorar la salud de esta población.

Nuestra investigación consistió de 606 entrevistados entre 18 y 65 año de edad. Siete por ciento de nuestros entrevistados padecen de diabetes, 61 porciento reportaron tener historia familiar de diabetes y cincuenta y nueve por ciento de nuestros entrevistados sufren de sobrepeso.

Algunos de los resultados que destacan en nuestra investigación son que existe una interacción deficiente entre sistema de salud y acciones de salud preventivas. Especialmente entre la población masculina, en la que sólo un 52 por ciento de ellos reportaron haberse hecho un examen de diabetes en los últimos 12 meses. Este resultado fue aun mas bajo entre hombres indocumentados, entre los cuales el 40 por ciento reportó haberse hecho un examen para detectar la diabetes.

La educación fue otro factor estadísticamente significativo entre nuestros resultados. Los entrevistados con menos años de educación representan menos probabilidad de utilizar los servicios de salud. Solamente un 39 por ciento de la población reportó haber recibido algún tipo de educación sobre la diabetes.

Encontramos que el estatus migratorio esta correlacionado con la probabilidad de recibir información acerca de la diabetes. Por ejemplo, solamente 3 de cada 10 migrantes reportaron haber recibido información acerca de la diabetes comparado a 5 de cada 10 de aquellos que no han migrado, y solamente 2 de cada 10 migrantes quienes son indocumentados reportaron haber recibido algún tipo de información sobre la diabetes.

En lo que respecta a la nutrición, el análisis por género mostró diferencias significativas en el consumo de granos, legumbres, y proteínas, siendo las mujeres quienes consumen más alimentos considerados protectores por especialistas en prevención de diabetes. El 21 por ciento de mujeres consumen, mientras que los hombres las consumen en un 13 por ciento. Las mujeres también consumen significativamente más productos lácteos (43%) que hombres (28%).

Al medir los niveles de actividad física, Los datos muestran que el 89,5 por ciento de los encuestados reportaron algún tipo de actividad física. Los hombres promediaron 335 minutos de actividad física en una semana, mientras que las mujeres lo hacen en promedio 192 minutos.

Los tlacuitapenses que viven en Estados Unidos hacen un poco más de actividad física que los no migrantes (280 minutos los primeros, y 231 los últimos). Un hallazgo sorprendente fue que la relación entre bienestar económico y la actividad física muestra una relación inversa, a mayor riqueza menor ejercicio.

Por los datos en relación a la dinámica con sistemas de salud, podemos concluir que como individuos biculturales, los migrantes se enfrentan a obstáculos para la comprensión, la interpretación y la colaboración con el sistema de salud en Estados Unidos, que es incapaz de atender sus necesidades además de subestimar o interpretar mal sus valores y creencias sobre la salud y la enfermedad. La información es una forma clave de la salud preventiva en la lucha contra las enfermedades crónicas. Los participantes de menor ingreso y educación, fueron los más propensos a no recibir información sobre la diabetes, así como los inmigrantes indocumentados en los EE.UU.

Esto puede influir en el proceso de toma de decisiones informadas de la búsqueda de atención médica y el cambio de los hábitos de nutrición y ejercicio para prevenir la enfermedad. Así, lo que sugiere la posibilidad de que los inmigrantes indocumentados con menos educación y menos ingresos no recibirán información sobre la diabetes no buscar atención preventiva para evitar la enfermedad.

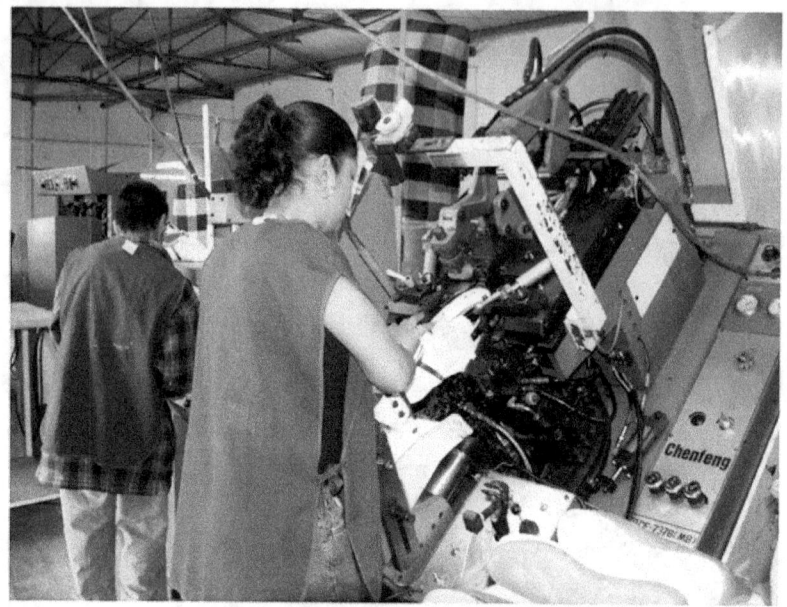

Tlacuitapense women at work in a shoe factory on the outskirts of Tlacuitapa. (Photo by Wayne Cornelius)

5 WORKPLACE HEALTH ON BOTH SIDES OF THE BORDER

CAMILA GAVIN BRAVO, TROY ARAIZA KOKINIS, MARISELA ORTÍZ, EMILY WILLIAMS, GUADALUPE ARCEO AND DEBRA CORNELIUS

> *Well, you know, I fell, and they wanted to fire me. When I suffered the fracture, [the supervisor] told me, "You work tomorrow or you don't have work." I had three days after the injury. So, I put my hand in a cast like this [demonstrating how he made a homemade cast]. And he told me, "You want to work?" And I said, "There is no problem; everything is fine."* —Juan, a 45-year-old man who fell off of a tractor due to a loose seat, was run over by the tractor, and fractured his arm while working in on a farm in the San Joaquin Valley, California.

In this chapter we compare employment-related health issues among residents of Tlacuitapa with those experienced by Tlacuitapenses living in the town's satellite communities in the United States. We ask: In which country, the United States or Mexico, are Tlacuitapenses safer in regards to their occupational health? To answer this question we focus on four key indicators — perceived safety of the workplace, experienced injuries and abuses, reported grievances, and sought medical treatment -- to construct a comprehensive picture of the factors that affect occupational health and safety.

Our analysis highlights common understandings and perceptions held by Tlacuitapenses and how they relate to actual rates of injuries and abuses. We also investigate patterns in reporting injuries and treatment for the injuries. We argue that occupational health wellness is better for men in Mexico while it is better for women in the United States. We reach this conclusion primarily based on the rates of injuries and abuses suffered in the United States, although Tlacuitapenses seem to be reporting and receiving treatment more often in the United States. However, after noting these differences we must also acknowledge that work life in both the United States and Tlacuitapa is harsh, for both men and women, though occupational health wellness does vary by location and by gender.

LITERATURE REVIEW

Existing research on migration and occupational health often limits the study population to one particular occupation, most commonly agricultural work (Sakala, 1987; Schenker & McCurdy, 1990; Mobed, Gold & Schenker, 1992; Stallones et al., 2009; McCauley, Langley & Rohlman, 2006). Most research in this field is also biased toward the male migrant workforce, by targeting certain "high-risk" occupations, such as agriculture and construction (Nissen, Angee & Weinstein, 2008; Welch et al., 2007). For example, in a study based on statistics from George Washington University Hospital, only 3 percent of the sample was female (Welch et al., 2005: 13). Other studies specifically target female-dominated occupations such as hotel service (see Buchanan et al., 2010; Krause et al., 2005). Research typically focuses solely on migrant occupational health risks on the U.S. side of the border (see Gleeson, 2010; Welch et al., 2005; Zhang, 2012). Binational comparisons are rare. Research often relies on aggregate statistics, often from Bureau of Labor Statistics (BLS), or only on qualitative data; a mixed-methods approach is seldo used. Finally, many quantitative studies, especially those using BLS statistics, offer vague demographic distinctions that are limited to "Latinos" or "Hispanics," which do not distinguish between immigrant and native-born workers.

Using a binational approach, our research is not limited to examining structural conditions solely in the United States or Mexico. We recognize that experiences on both sides of the border affect perceptions and behavior. Moreover, our sample includes a wide range of occupations, representing both men and women, which is more representative of the rural population in Mexico as a whole. Finally, by giving women equal attention, we do not confine our analysis of occupational health in the Mexican migrant community to male workers in the United States. Instead, we are able to paint a more comprehensive and clearer picture of the occupational health conditions of women in a Mexican high-emigration town.

Injuries and Abuse Rates

Published studies consistently state that Latinos and migrants suffer high rates of occupational injuries. Schenker (2008) notes that Latinos make up 10.2 percent of the US workforce, but 17.1 percent of occupational injuries and illnesses. He notes that Latinos disproportionately work in high-risk occupations: construction, agriculture, transportation and housekeeping. Migrant workers suffer a disproportionate amount of injuries in the United States compared to other workers in the United States, pattern that seems to persist even when examining demographics within the same U.S.-based occupation. Orrenius and Zavodny (2009) demonstrate that the proportion of fatal workplace injuries being suffered among immigrants is on the rise. They also attribute this to that fact that immigrants are disproportionately employed in high-risk jobs (Orrenius and Zavodny 2009). According to Welch, Hunting, and Murawski (2005), the most common types of injuries are suffered primarily in construction, with 34 percent due to contact with objects, 21 percent due to falls, and 20 percent due to over-exertion.

In both qualitative and quantitative studies of migrants' occupational health, little attention is devoted to physical and psychological abuse suffered by workers. A major exception is the work of Seth Holmes (2011, 2013), who uses ethnographic methods to lay out the power dynamic between workers and management on a large-scale berry farm in Washington. Holmes sees mistreatment of the migrant workforce as a symptom of the "structural vulnerability" of the entire farm in the face of a competitive global market. Thus, all who are involved with the farm, from the owners to the pickers, suffer from the uncertainty of the market, and the migrant field workers often bear the worst of these structural pressures. Holmes argues that indigenous Mexican workers on small farms suffer the worst abuses in global agribusiness, since they are on the bottom of the totem pole on the farm, in a business that is at the towards the bottom of the global market.

Walter et al. (2002) touch upon verbal abuse in the workplace, describing a case of a worker who was insulted by the boss after being hurt on the job. Krause, Schrezer and Rugulies (2005) discuss cases in which workers in a

Las Vegas hotel have been compelled to work through their break hours. In a study of undocumented and trafficked workers in San Diego, in which 98 percent of the sample is Mexican, Zhang (2012) notes that undocumented construction workers suffer the highest rates of abusive labor practices (63 percent reported such abuse), while those working in the janitorial and cleaning businesses come in second with 59 percent.

Perceptions of Work and the Workplace in the United States

According to Shannon Gleeson, undocumented migrants are more inclined to accept abuse from employers and hard working conditions because they view their time in the United States as temporary; undocumented status leaves migrants with a short-term understanding of their working life in the U.S. (Gleeson 2010: 561). Gordon and Lenhardt (2008: 1185-1210) point to a structural source of such acceptance of hardship: the importance of "hard work" to a "civic" conception of citizenship, which allows one to belong to the wider United States community.

Stallones et al. (2009) explore the social, cultural, and health and safety beliefs of farmworkers who have migrated to Colorado from México, and of those who have never migrated working in Guanajuato, Mexico by noting differences in perception of the workplace between the two countries: Provision of adequate protective equipment was important to fewer workers in Mexico because of the need to provide and pay for it out of pocket. Pesticides were viewed by participants as being better regulated in the United States than in Mexico, with the chemicals in Mexico seen as being stronger. Colorado-based workers reported a willingness to seek medical treatment in the United States but would return to Mexico for extensive treatment. Overall, migrant workers, especially those who are undocumented, demonstrate very high levels of tolerance for workplace incidents and have very low expectations for employers.

Reporting of Work-Related Injuries

While working in the United States, undocumented workers try to avoid any confrontation with employers. According to Gleeson, their reasoning is twofold: 1) Many fear retribution by an employer, specifically firing or deportation, and 2) others have a calculated plan for their time in the US, and "choose not to deploy their knowledge of workplace rights in order to maintain a modicum of certainty in their lives" (Gleeson 2010: 582-583).

Welch, Hunting, and Murawski (2007: 39) discuss how the apparent decrease in injury and illness rates in construction may actually be a result of "changes in the ways injuries are treated, misclassification of employees, or underreporting". Welch and colleagues comment on the role of employers in reporting and specifically the role of employers misclassifying workers and how that has skewed the BLS data on workplace injury and illness to be much lower than it is in reality. This is important because when workers report to their employers about injuries and illnesses, employers are supposed to file those claims with worker's compensation, yet Welch et al demonstrate how the misclassification workers as independent contractors is used as a loophole to avoid providing compensation.

The trends in reporting can also be linked to perceptions held by migrant workers in the United States. As most do not view their situations as permanent, they do not see it worth their time and energy to seek justice and compensation for work-related torment. Court processes for claiming compensation in the United States are often long and bureaucratic, and at home in Mexico workers often do not report injuries either.

Treatment of Work-Related Inquiries

Existing literature is limited by its reliance on national-level government statistics, which make it quite difficult to quantify how many injuries took place across the country without being treated. Thus, most investigations remain focused on case studies, and they find that most migrant workers in the United States receive treatment for work-related injuries. However, a large proportion do not receive proper treatment, due to failure to report the injury and/or lack of sufficient knowledge about where to go to receive compensation for treatment.

In a study of traumatic injuries in Washington state, 27 percent of injuries did not list Workers' Compensation as a payer, while 37 percent did not have a claim filed with Workers' Compensation (Sears et al., 2013). In California, only half of farmworkers received medical attention after an occupational injury (Hoerster et al., 2011). In a survey of 427 Latino immigrant workers in Arlandia, Virginia, only 20 percent of respondents claimed to have health insurance, 27 percent paid for medical care on their own, 6 percent sought care at a free clinic, and 2 percent sought care through Medicaid. Moreover, 21 percent of respondents reported not knowing what to do if they suffered a workplace injury, and 56 percent of respondents were told by their employers that they were not covered for healthcare through workers' compensation (Pransky et al., 2011). In a Colorado case study, workers reported a willingness to seek medical treatment in the United States, but would return to Mexico for extensive treatment (Stallones et al., 2009). Overall, migrant workers seem to suffer from a lack of information on how to report injuries and seek compensation for medical treatment of injuries — most likely due to a combination of communication barriers and employer/employee ambivalence.

WORK IN TLACUITAPA

Tlacuitapenses often struggle to find year-round work in their home town. Work in Tlacuitapa primarily consists of temporary or seasonal jobs in construction and agriculture, done mostly by men, and factory production which is dominated by women. In Tlacuitapa, 38 percent of the male workforce is employed in agriculture. Since the implementation of the North American Free Trade Agreement in 1994, small-scale Mexican farmers have been deeply affected, and Tlacuitapenses are no exception. In a 2007 MMFRP survey, 60 percent of Tlacuitapenses reported that NAFTA had had damaging effects on their community. In addition, some farmers from Tlacuitapa specifically blamed NAFTA for their inability to continue working in agriculture (Cantú, Shaiq and Urdanivia, 2007). Partly as a consequence of NAFTA-related competition, and partly due to the dismantling of agricultural subsidies by Mexico's technocratic governments since the late 1980s, agricultural work in Tlacuitapa has decreased in recent decades.

Construction is the second most common source of employment for men in Tlacuitapa, with 15 percent of men working in that sector. Construction work in the town is typically funded by a migrant based in the United States who hires a Tlacuitapense back home to work on a home-building or remodeling project. Labor relations in such projects are extremely informal. No contracts are signed and employers often remain in the United States while a supervisor (usually a family member or friend) manages the construction project in Tlacuitapa. As 58-year-old Eduardo explained, "They leave someone in charge. Or many come now for a month or something and then they leave, and they halt the project and then when they come again, they work on it again." As a result, the local construction market depends primarily on remittances from the United States, which tend to fall in periods of economic distress in the United States.

Many people in Tlacuitapa do not work under an employer and instead work for themselves or own their own business (45 percent). This is most commonly seen in agriculture, where 57 percent of people do not work under an employer. In addition, 60 percent of those who work in stores or other forms of commerce either work for themselves or have their own business. This high rate of self-employment is important. People who work for themselves are significantly less likely to suffer a work-related injury, since they have more decision-making power in the workplace. Additionally, they are at no risk of suffering workplace abuse, as they can avoid the possibility of working under an abusive boss.

The majority of women in Tlacuitapa – 60 percent – are economically inactive and work only in the home. After marrying, most women in Tlacuitapa become housewives, while women who work outside the home in Tlacuitapa tend to be young and unmarried or widowed. Of those women in the workforce, 11 percent work in sales or in stores, and 6 percent of women in Tlacuitapa work in a local shoe factory. Though only 6 percent of the female labor force currently works in the factory, many of the town's young women have worked in the shoe factory at some point. In total, 9 percent female Tlacuitapenses have worked in the factory, which equates to roughly one-quarter of the working female population. The factory has very high turn-over rates, most likely related to dangerous labor conditions and a high prevalence of workplace abuse.

Tlacuitapa's shoe factory opened in 2004, with assistance from the state and federal governments. The building that houses the factory previously served as a warehouse for CONASUPO, a Mexican paraestatal enterprise that once regulated markets of staple foods and for low-income families (Yunez-Naude, 2003). The shoe factory inherited the building rent free, as part of a federal privatization program that brought about the national-level dismantling of CONASUPO. The company that owns the factory, located in the adjoining state of Guanajuato, established the factory in Tlacuitapa to utilize the town's supply of cheap, readily available labor without competition from other industries. The factory receives a government subsidy to pay workers $450 for a week of training, after which they are meant to receive a wage of approximately $250 per week, though they typically end up with far less (Cantú, Shaiq and Urdanivia, 2007). The vulnerability of workers in Tlacuitapa's shoe factory is illustrated by Patricia, a 21-year-old factory worker, who told us: "They [the factory managers] know that whatever they do, they can do it because we are not going to do anything, because there's no other work for us to do."

WORK IN THE UNITED STATES

The majority of Tlacuitapenses who migrate to the United States go to either Oklahoma City, Oklahoma or Union City, California. In both locations, Tlacuitapenses are concentrated primarily in four industries: construction, agriculture, manufacturing and service work. In Oklahoma City, the majority of men work in construction, while in Union City men have a wider range of jobs. In Union City, women are concentrated primarily in services, while in Oklahoma City their jobs are more diverse. Moreover, Tlacuitapenses are significantly more likely to work under an employer in the United States rather than independently. Only 5 percent of those working in the United States are self-employed or own their business.

A majority of male Tlacuitapense migrants in the United States -- 59 percent -- work in construction. In the United States, construction projects are typically large-scale, which entails a higher likelihood of injury than those in Tlacuitapa. Many U.S.-based migrants work for a Tlacuitapense who owns a construction firm in Oklahoma City, where they work on public works projects, specifically bridge-building. Moreover, construction in the United States tends be more specialized than in Tlacuitapa. Although most construction workers in the United States have formal contracts, semi-formal and informal labor still exists, primarily among undocumented workers. Smaller shares of Tlacuitapense migrants to the United States work in manufacturing (12 percent), and agriculture (4 percent).

In Union City and Oklahoma City, female migrants primarily work in factories (11 percent) and domestic services (12 percent). Again, a plurality of women (41 percent) work strictly in the home. However, more Tlacuitapense women in the United States have joined the workforce, and their occupations are much more diversified than those of male migrants. Eugenia, who lives in Union City, California, has worked several jobs since she migrated from Tlacuitapa. Her first job was cleaning houses; she currently works at a Wal-Mart store. Due to the higher cost of living there, more Tlacuitapense women living in the United States are likely to work outside of the home.

DESCRIPTIVE STATISTICS

Our survey results demonstrate that occupational health is better for those who work in Mexico than for those working in the United States. We begin by exploring injury and abuse rates, and then examine other behaviors that are related to occupational health wellness, such as perceptions, reporting and treatment. Again, we emphasize that although Tlacuitapenses are statistically safer working in Mexico, this does not negate the fact that a significantly high number of work-related incidents take place there, too.

Injury Rates

Tlacuitapenses experience higher rates of workplace injuries in the United States than in Mexico. Of those working in Mexico, 14.9 percent have suffered a workplace injury causing at least one week to be missed of work, while twice as many – 28 percent – of those working in the United States have suffered such an injury. In both the United States and Mexico, Tlacuitapenses average roughly two work-related injuries throughout their lifetime.

We found that occupational health varies by gender on both sides of the border. As shown in Table 5.1, men are significantly more susceptible to occupational injuries in the United States than in Mexico. The majority of males in the United States are employed in high-risk occupations, such as construction and agriculture, and 95 percent of the workforce is employed under a boss. If they remain in Tlacuitapa, women are likely to have spent at least some time working in the high-risk shoe factory, though the majority of women in the town are amas de casa (60 percent). In the United States, Tlacuitapense women often work service jobs that may carry a high risk but are less risky than jobs in construction. Only 41 percent of female migrants in the United States are economically inactive.

Table 5.1 Injuries Reported, by Gender and Work Location

	United States	Mexico	Workforce injured (Total)
Male	34.4%	14.8%	14%
Female	14.3%	14.4%	6%

In Mexico, the most common injuries suffered by Tlacuitapenses are falls (28.8 percent), back pains (19.2 percent) and cuts (19.2 percent). Figure 5.1 shows the distribution of types of workplace injuries suffered by Tlacuitapenses while working in Mexico, by occupation. Factory and construction workers have suffered the highest proportions of injuries in Mexico, at one-third of the total workforce respectively. Among those who have experienced falls in the workplace, one-third worked in construction and another third worked in services. Among those who have experienced back pains, 38.5 percent worked in a factory and 30.8 percent worked in service occupations. Among those who have experienced cuts, 33.3 percent worked in manufacturing a factory and 33.3 percent worked in construction.

Figure 5.1 Types of Workplace Injuries, by Occupation in Mexico

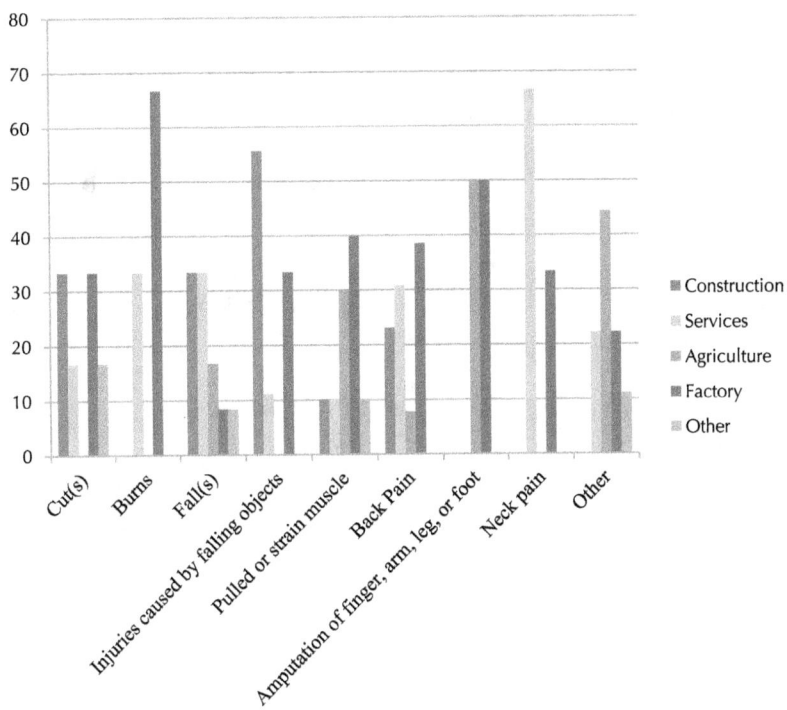

One-third of the manufacturing workforce in Mexico has suffered injuries. Angelina, a 40-year-old woman who worked in the shoe factory, reported a serious workplace injury that led to the amputation of two of her fingers: "My hand got stuck under a hot machine for around three minutes. I screamed until a man came to get it off of me, and afterward a doctor had to amputate two fingers." When asked how many injuries she had suffered while working at the shoe factory, Rosa, a 39-year-old mother of two, replied: "My back has hurt every single day since beginning to work there!" Lola, a 42-year-old woman who lives in Tlacuitapa,told us about an injury she had suffered while working in the shoe factory: "While attempting to retrieve more fabric from the top section of a fabric display, I fell to the ground and I broke my arm." Although many women in Tlacuitapa remain housewives, those who work have very few options for employment, hence the high proportion of injuries suffered in the shoe factory.

In the United States, the most common injuries suffered by Tlacuitapenses are falls (28.8 percent), injuries caused by falling objects (21.9 percent), and back pains (19.2 percent). Figure 5.2 shows the distribution of workplace injuries that Tlacuitapenses have experienced while working in the United States by occupation. Among those who have experienced falls, 38.1 percent worked in construction and 19 percent worked in the service industry. Among those who suffered an injury caused by a falling object, 56.2 percent worked in construction and 18.2 percent worked in services. Among those who had experienced back pains, 71.4 percent worked in construction and 21.4 percent worked in a manufacturing job.

Figure 5.2 Types of Workplace Injuries in the United States, by Occupation

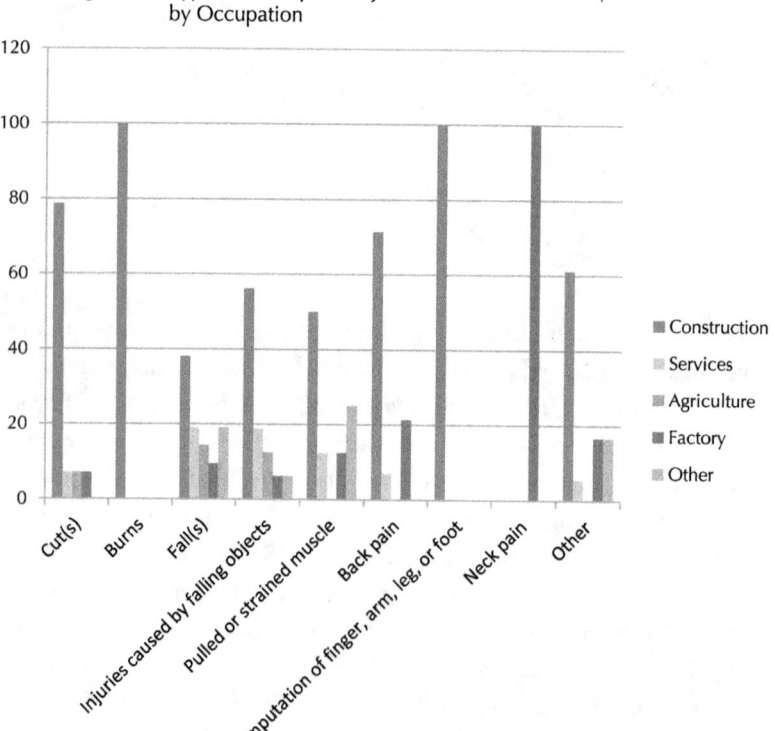

Construction workers in the United States experience far more workplace injuries compared to other occupations. More than three-quarters (78.6 percent) of construction workers have suffered injuries at work. Because construction is primarily a male-dominated industry, men experience more workplace injuries in the United States than in Mexico. Rafael, a 54-year-old man who lives in Oklahoma City, reported an injury that he experienced while working in construction: "My supervisor told us to carry very heavy pieces of cement. When I was carrying one of the pieces, I hurt my back. My doctor said that I pulled a muscle. I couldn't return to work for three months because every time I moved my body, it hurt a lot!" Jorge Luis, a 34-year-old man who lives in Oklahoma City, has also experienced back pain due to work: "Carrying all the heavy equipment takes a toll on you. I have to take pain medication to work because my back hurts all the time ... .Without the medicine, I can't work right."

Abuse Rates

Rates of workplace abuse are high for Tlacuitapenses working on both sides of the border. When considering gender, 30 percent of men and 38 percent of women in Mexico have suffered abuse at the workplace, compared to the United States where 35 percent of men and 17 percent of women have experienced abuse.

Wage theft and verbal abuse are the most common types of abuses suffered by Tlacuitapenses in both the United States and Mexico. Wage theft occurs when a worker is not paid at all, or is not paid the full amount of their wages for work performed, including unpaid overtime. As shown in Table 5.2, among interviewees who work in Tlacuitapa, 12 percent of men and 20 percent of women reported that they had experienced wage theft, compared to 14 percent of men and 26 percent of women in the United States who reported this type of abuse.

Table 5.2 Wage Theft by Work Location and Gender

	Male	Female	Workers affected (Total)
United States	14%	26%	10%
Mexico	12%	20%	16%

In Mexico, manufacturing workers have suffered the highest proportion of wage theft, at 30 percent. Patricia, a 21-year-old factory worker related her experience:

> They were going to pay us and the person in charge gave us our checks. When we opened them, we noticed that they had taken out money. We noticed because the checks come in an envelope and a paper comes on top and there is a staple and when they gave us the checks, we noticed that the staples had been removed and that the papers had then been re-stapled. We got mad and we began to tell him and he said yes, that he had done it.

Tlacuitapa-based construction workers also suffer a relatively high proportion of wage theft, at 15 percent. Jaime explained how he suffered wage theft while working for a small construction company in the town:

> When the boss got some money from a job he gave some of it to us on Saturdays. He would then give us the rest of the money that he owed us at mid-week. But one time he seemed nervous. He gave us some of our money on Saturday but at mid-week he was quiet. We waited and we said, "Oh, Saturday he will give us the rest of what he owes us." But he didn't. He only gave us only what he owed us for that week.

In the United States, Tlacuitapenses working in manufacturing experience the highest rates of wage theft (31 percent), while 14 percent of domestic service workers and 12 percent of agricultural and construction workers, respectively, have been victims as well. Miguel, a construction worker from Oklahoma, claimed that workers often suffer from wage theft while working on public works projects. He recognizes that the state pays contractors prevailing wages, which are dictated by the Davis-Bacon Act of 1931 for federally funded projects like the construction of bridges and roads. However, contractors will often pay workers significantly less and skim the extra amount for themselves.

Both men and women increase their risk of wage theft while working in the United States. Undocumented migrants are particularly susceptible to wage theft because they typically work informal jobs and are too afraid to confront their employer, or contact the labor commission, due to fear of deportation. Language barriers also make it easier for employers to not pay migrant workers, documented or undocumented, as employers can easily take advantage of a "misunderstanding" regarding owed wages, and workers often do not feel confident enough to confront their employers if they have poor English language skills.

Rates of wage theft are quite difficult to capture because workers often do not know when it has occurred. Moreover, many do not recognize wage theft as a problem due to how frequently it occurs – instead, it is seen as "part of business." In our survey, respondents were asked if have ever suffered "wage theft" without always being given a clear definition of the meaning of the term. Therefore we believe that stolen wages are underreported in our sample.

Verbal abuse is the second most common type of abuse suffered by Tlacuitapenses on both sides of the border. Roughly 11 percent of the male workforce in Mexico has experienced verbal abuse, compared to 15 percent of those who work in the United States. Among female workers, 8 percent of those based in Tlacuitapa have experienced verbal abuse, compared with 6 percent of female U.S.-based workers.

In Mexico, those who work in agriculture and manufacturing suffer the highest rate of verbal abuse, at 9 percent. Patricia, a factory worker in Tlacuitapa, reported the verbal abuse that she suffers from one of the factory's supervisors: "Sometimes he speaks to us badly, sometimes he even yells at us. We will be sitting there and first he will speak to us and then he will start yelling at us and everyone hears it. He has a very strong character."

In the United States, 9 percent of construction workers and 8 percent of manufacturing workers have suffered verbal abuse. Enrique, who works in a salt refinery in Union City, describes his boss' reply after he told him that a task he was asked to perform was unsafe: "He said, 'Look, I don't give a shit what you think but that fucking job has to be done." Juan, a Tlacuitapense who used to work in agriculture in the San Joaquin Valley, observed that undocumented migrants often suffer the most from verbal abuse. He reported: "If you are illegal, you can't speak. They [the bosses] shout, 'if you're not happy, leave or we can deport you'".

Some Tlacuitapenses have experienced physical or other types of violence at the hands of their employers. In the United States, 8 percent of men and 9 percent of women reported physical abuse by an employer, compared to 3 percent of men and 1 percent of women in Mexico. In Tlacuitapa, Carla witnessed an act of violence while she was working as a house cleaner. She recalled that one of her co-workers was hit by the employer after the employer blamed her for losing the remote control to a television.

Perceptions of Work and Workplace Safety

A high proportion of Tlacuitapenses have favorable perceptions of their employers. In our survey we asked, "How important is it to your employer that workers are not put at risk of occupational injury?" Responses were overwhelmingly positive, as 73.3 percent of workers in Mexico responded "very" or "somewhat important," and 71.8 percent of workers in the United States who responded similarly.

However, some differences emerge when looking at gender. Females employed in Mexico are most likely to recognize their dangerous working conditions, with 31.1 percent of them reporting that reducing workplace risk is only "somewhat" or "not important" to their employer. This probably reflects the fact that one-quarter of the economically active female population of Tlacuitapa works under dangerous manufacturing conditions.. Males who work in the United States are most likely to perceive that their employers take care not to put them at risk. The overwhelming majority (86 percent) reported that their employer considers it "somewhat or very important" to reduce workplace risks. Ironically, more than one-third (34.4 percent) of Tlacuitapense men working in the United States reported sustaining an occupational injury or illness that caused them to miss a week or more of work.

Such perceptions suggest a disconnect among many workers, between what they believe their employer thinks in regard to employees' safety and actual hazards in the workplace, as measured by the number of injuries sustained there. But when those who had suffered an occupational injury were asked how they thought their employers viewed workplace safety, they often answered that their employers were not concerned about safety. For example, when asked about an employer's concern for his workers, Ivan, a man who fell while working construction in Tlacuitapa, answered, "Here there is no insurance, nothing. Nobody here cares about the worker here, not at all."

When asked whether or not it is important to their employer that workers are given adequate safety training and equipment, 82.7 percent of males working in the United States and 78.1 percent of women working in that country responded that they thought it is somewhat or very important to their employers. When asked the same question, 76.3 percent of working males in Mexico and 70.1 percent of employed females in Mexico answered that it is somewhat to very important to their employer that they are provided with adequate safety equipment and training. These perceptions suggest that workers internalize the responsibility for preventing workplace accidents, placing the burden on themselves rather than on the employer. They may also hesitate to question the good intentions of their employer, out of a fear of retaliation.

While there have been attempts to organize workers in Tlacuitapa, especially among women working in manufacturing, the threat of repercussions eventually deterred workers from organizing. Patricia, a young woman working in the shoe factory in Tlacuitapa, was asked whether workers have ever tried to organize to pressure their supervisor. She answered:

> Yes, we came together and talked and agreed that we were going to do something, but after he found out that we were trying to organize ourselves he made us come to his office and told us, 'don't throw a fit'. The workers were very excited to do something and then he says things to them so that they don't do anything. They [the workers] get scared and don't do anything.

In this instance, employer intimidation played a key role in deterring the workers from organizing themselves. This, in combination with the lack of employment opportunities in the town, leaves workers largely unable to defend themselves.

In one exceptional case, a construction worker in Tlacuitapa successfully organized a walk-out with his co-workers after the boss failed to pay them roughly half of their earned wages. Jaime explained why it is important to organize with co-workers: "If only you, one person, leave, [the employer] is not going to care … nothing will happen. But if you're united with your co-workers and you leave, then the boss may do something."

Reporting of Work-Related Injuries

Tlacuitapenses are much more likely to report workplace-related injuries in the United States than in Mexico, even though they often do not report to the proper authorities. Among male Tlacuitapenses working in the United States, only 4 percent did not report their injuries to anyone, while 9 percent of females did not report. By contrast, of those injured in Mexico, 36 percent of both males and females failed to report their injuries to anyone.

In the United States, Tlacuitapenses often do not report their injuries to government agencies, such as OSHA, and/or to labor unions, which can demand long-term structural change in the workplace. Instead, they report only to their employers, who can shove the incident under the table. Often, this results in the worker receiving employer-funded treatment for their injuries, but it enables a culture of poor occupational health to persist in the workplace due to a failure to change practices and a lack of oversight. For example, Efrain was working with heavy machinery in Oklahoma when an object hit him in the eye. He told his employer, who took him to the hospital, paid for his treatment, and compensated his time off. But he did not file any official documentation of the incident. In these types of cases, immediate treatment for the worker at the time of the injury is seen by employers as the less costly alternative, compared with filing legal documentation and having to change labor practices within the firm.

Of those who did not report their injury to anyone, when asked why, Tlacuitapenses on both sides of the border said they did not report because they did not believe their injury to be serious. Among those injured in Mexico, 37.5 percent gave this explanation, while 50 percent of those injured in the United States gave the same response. Since any type of occupational injury that occurs in high-risk jobs should be addressed, failure to report an injury due to the perception that it is not serious could be reflective of a larger lack of faith in the institutions that can exact larger, structural change.

Treatment of Work-Related Inquiries

The majority of Tlacuitapenses in both Mexico (89 percent) and the United States (93 percent) have received treatment after a work-related injury that caused them to miss a week or more of work. Emergency rooms and hospitals, clinics and private doctors are the most common places where Tlacuitapenses sought treatment. In addition, there is very little difference in the types of treatment sought between men and women, in either location.

In Tlacuitapa, a large proportion of those who suffered an occupational injury (19 percent) sought treatment at an emergency room or hospital. Ruben described the treatment he received at a governmental hospital in Mexico after hurting his hand working in agriculture: "At the hospital they told me that my hand didn't work, but only three of my fingers were injured. It's just that at governmental hospitals, it is easier for them to cut it. At that hospital they didn't want to fight for my hand at all, the easiest thing for them is it to cut it off and since people don't know and they're in pain, they tell them to do what they need to do." Ruben believes that if he had been able to seek care from a private hospital or doctor, that his hand would have been saved. However, seeking treatment from a private doctor is expensive and most people are unable to afford it. Only 3 percent of our respondents in Tlacuitapa received treatment from a private doctor after a work-related injury. Eleven percent did not receive any treatment at all for their injury.

In the United States, Tlacuitapenses are more than twice as likely to receive medical attention at an emergency room or hospital than in Mexico. This is likely due to the risky nature of the work that Tlacuitapenses typically perform in the United States, especially in construction, which has the potential to result in more serious injuries. Rodrigo explained why it was imperative that he seek treatment after he suffered a back injury while doing some heavy lifting in Oklahoma: "I started to feel bad, like it was really hot. Like when the heat hurts you, a wave of heat. I went to emergency." Eight percent of Tlacuitapenses working in the United States went to a private doctor, while seven percent did not receive any type of treatment for their occupational injury.

After suffering a work-related injury, 23 percent of Tlacuitapenses in the United States paid out of their own pocket for medical attention compared to 11 percent in Mexico. Though our respondents paid. on average. more money out of pocket in the United States than in Mexico, they are paying far less of a proportion of their U.S.-earned income. While in the United States our respondents paid 25 percent of their total weekly income out of pocket after an occupational injury, those in Mexico paid 74 percent. Furthermore, men are more likely to pay more money out of pocket in Mexico while women are more likely to pay more in the United States. Herman, a construction worker in Tlacuitapa who worked under an absentee employer who lived in the United States, broke his hand after falling from the second story of a house. After his injury, he had to pay the full amount to the doctor. His supervisor paid him two weeks of extra wages, but he had to miss three months of work as a result.

Fortunately, the vast majority of Tlacuitapenses are receiving medical treatment for their occupational injuries on both sides of the border. It is important to note that although Tlacuitapenses in the United States are receiving treatment more often, and paying a smaller proportion of their treatment expenses out of pocket, they are still paying out of their own pocket more frequently than their Tlacuitapa-based counterparts, and are being injured at twice the rate.

CONSEQUENCES OF OCCUPATIONAL (UN)HEALTH

Poor occupational health conditions have produced a variety of negative consequences for Tlacuitapenses on both sides of the border. As summarized in Figure 5.3, these consequences include being unable to work due to disability, having to change jobs or go into debt, being compelled to migrate, and becoming homeless.

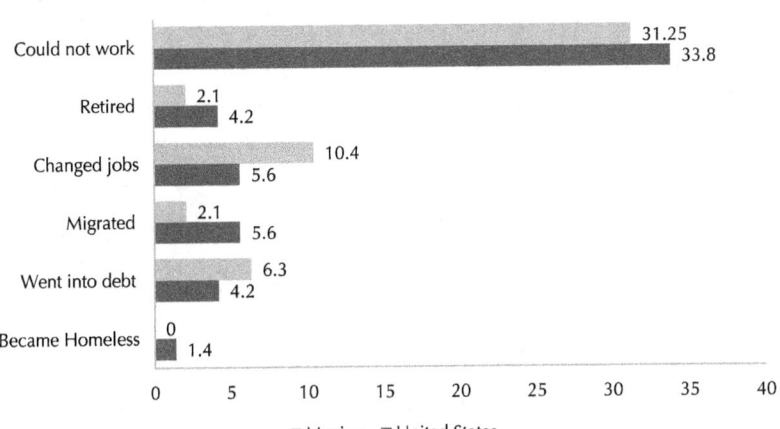

Figure 5.3 Consequences of Occupational (Un)health, by Place of Residence

After a workplace-related incident in the United States, many workers have been forced to return to Mexico. While working in a printing plant in the United States, Ramón suffered a back injury that prevented him from working for nearly a year, during which he was searching for a new, less physically demanding job. Toward the end of his year-long quest, unable to find work, Ramón began feeling very depressed and returned to Mexico. His experience with depression is not uncommon. Ten percent of Tlacuitapenses reported feelings of depression due to a work-related incident in the United States, while 6.2 percent of workers have felt depressed due to work in Mexico.

In another case, Rodrigo, an undocumented Tlacuitapense who hurt his knee while working in a warehouse in Hayward, California, underwent five surgeries and was out of work for nine years. For seven of these years he was paid 80 percent of his salary, but sometimes he would go months without receiving any compensation. As a result, Rodrigo had to borrow money from family remembers and ended up deeply in debt. He eventually received $36,000 in compensation after hiring a lawyer, to whom he paid $8,000.

Occupational injuries have also resulted in homelessness. Jorge, a 23-year-old construction worker interviewed in Oklahoma, worked for a contractor on a project for nearly two months but did not get paid. As a result of being owed nearly $3,000 in wages, he could no longer afford the room that he rented in a house where twelve immigrant workers lived. He went homeless for three weeks and survived on food donations from the community, which he received by going door-to-door.

In extreme cases, victims of workplace injuries suffer lasting results that have transformed their everyday lives. Israel, a 34-year-old worker who lost half of his arm while working in agriculture in Tlacuitapa, feels that people discriminate against him because he is missing his arm. He continues to seek work in agriculture due to his background and skill set. Regardless of his disability, he intends to return to the United States without documents in order to raise money to pay his child's medical bills.

Another example of an occupational injury having life-long consequences was provided by Miguel, who suffered a brain aneurism after being struck by a falling object while working construction in Union City. Doctors expected that he would be paralyzed with a 75 percent brain loss. Although he significantly recovered from the accident, he has not been able to return to work, and has since suffered from three major depressions. As a result of his experience, he has become active in the union movement in California, as a Field Representative for the Laborers' International Union.

CONCLUSION

In this chapter we have examined workplace health issues in Tlacuitapa and its satellite communities in the United States. We conclude that Tlacuitapenses' perceptions of their employers and workplace safety conditions are similar on both sides of the border, though men in the United States have the most positive perceptions and women in Mexico perceive their employers and safety conditions most negatively. The proportion of male workers injured in the United States (34 percent) is more than double the proportion of those injured in Tlacuitapa (14 percent). Rates of work-related injuries among women working on both sides are similar, at approximately 14 percent. In both Mexico and the United States, work-related injuries among Tlacuitapenses are the result of employment in high-risk occupations, social isolation, and larger structural pressures.

Some of the most dramatic effects of poor occupational health in Tlacuitapa relate directly to the town's depressed agricultural economy. In the past few years, there have reportedly been seven suicides in the town. Juan, a 59-year-old carpenter who has migrated to the United States four times without documents, explained:

> It is because they do not have any work here. They have no fun. There is no park. Nothing. There is nothing in Tlacuitapa. We are very desperate to work. The young people do not have futures. I am very scared for my daughters. I do not want them to go to El Norte.

Juan's testimony illustrates the frustration felt by many Tlacuitapenses regarding the few employment options offered Tlacuitapa's economy. Women are the most limited in their employment options, which is why so many resort to working in the shoe factory.

In regard to work-related abuses, men suffer more abuses in the United States, at 35 percent of the workforce, compared with 30 percent of males who have suffered abuses while working in Tlacuitapa. Among women, 17 percent have suffered abuses while working in the United States while more than double (38 percent) have suffered from abuses while working in Tlacuitapa. Rates of wage theft are higher for both men and women in the United States than in Mexico. Tlacuitapenses report their occupational injuries more often in the United States but often do not report accidents or abuses to the proper authorities. Most Tlacuitapenses receive treatment for workplace injuries on both sides of the border, though rates of treatment are slightly higher in the United States.

Overall, Tlacuitapense men working in the United States experience the highest rates of injuries and abuses, yet they also believe their U.S. employers value workplace safety more than do employers in Mexico. Women working in Tlacuitapa suffer abuses at higher rates than their counterparts in the United States, and they also believe that their employers value workplace safety much less than employers in the United States.

We suspect that rates of work-related disabilities among Tlacuitapenses are higher than reflected in our survey results. This is particularly true for those who suffer from chronic pain, since many times this pain does not result in missed days of work. We encountered numerous cases of such disabilities in our qualitative interviews. For example, Eugenia, a Wal-Mart worker in Union City, suffers from pain in her hand but has not missed any work as a result of the pain. She explained: "Because I hang clothes so much, my hand hurts." She notes that the pain is particularly bad in the winter months, when she has to hang clothes that are heavier and the weather is colder. Similarly, our survey does not capture work-place related deaths, one of which was reported by an interviewee in the United States.

We suggest that future research examine the role of occupational health in the decision to migrate. As reported above, 5.6 percent of Tlacuitapenses in the United States, and 2.1 percent of those interviewed in Mexico, migrated as a result of a work-related injury. Evidence from our qualitative interviews suggests that local working conditions and abuses play a role in decisions to migrate. Future research should also delve more deeply into the post-migration consequences of workplace injuries in the United States, and the role that injuries play in return migration, if any.

Our research suggests that education and better enforcement of workers' rights could help to improve the occupational health of Tlacuitapenses on both sides of the border. In the United States, a comprehensive legalization program would serve to improve migrant occupational health. Legalization would make workers less fearful of employer retaliation for reporting workplace hazards and make it easier for immigrants to challenge employers when believing themselves to be at occupational health risk. Legalization would also facilitate the unionization of immigrant workers, which has the potential to significantly improve labor conditions in numerous industries, since unionized workers tend to have better knowledge of workplace rights and legal processes.

In Tlacuitapa, the use of formal labor contracts and the enforcement of these contracts could serve to improve occupational health in the town. Unionization also has the potential to facilitate better labor conditions. In addition, workers in Tlacuitapa could try to mobilize the community as a mutual aid resource to improve workplace health conditions. Town residents are generally aware of the struggles of some workers against abusive employers but thus far have not participated in any collective action. More generally, Tlacuitapa residents could benefit from the development of agricultural production cooperatives, using pooled remittances from the United States. At present Tlacuitapenses do not benefit from a local agricultural surplus, but cooperatives could reverse this and create alternatives to emigration.[1]

Finally, we concur with Holmes (2011: 447) that "risk and risk behaviors" in health and medicine often carry the assumption that the individual is at fault for not properly preventing certain health conditions. This approach places blame on the victim, or the victim's culture, for "structurally produced suffering." We see the poor occupational health conditions of many Tlacuitapenses as a result of structural pressures that are inevitably found in production for a globalized market. Tlacuitapenses serve as a transnational working class that fulfills the cheap labor requirements of remaining competitive within this market. Thus, in a larger sense, Tlacuitapenses' poor occupational health can be viewed as just one of the negative consequences of being a disempowered, transnational underclass.

REFERENCES

Buchanan, S., Vossenas, P., Krause, N., Moriarty, J., Frumin, E., Shimek, J.A.M., Mirer, F., Orris, P., and Punnett, L. (2010). Occupational Injury Disparities in the US Hotel Industry. *American Journal of Industrial Medicine,* 53(2), 116–125.

Cantú, B., Shaiq F., and Urdanivia, A. (2007). Migration and Local Development. In Cornelius, W.A., and Lewis, J.M. (eds.). (129-147). Impacts of Border Enforcement on Mexican Migration: The View from Sending Communities. La Jolla, CA, and Boulder, CO: Center

---

1. The Andalusian town of Marinaleda offers an example of this approach to stimulating the economy of a depressed rural region prone to immigration. Before 1992 Marinaleda's inhabitants migrated to Germany and France for seasonal work in wheat fields. But after converting 1,200 hectares of municipal land to cooperative farming, the town now boasts full employment, while the current unemployment rate in Andalucia as a whole is 34 percent (Hancox, 2012).

for Comparative Immigration Studies, University of California-San Diego, and Lynne Rienner Publishers.

Gleeson, S. (2010). Labor Rights for All? The Role of Undocumented Immigrant Status for Worker Claims-Making. Law & Social Inquiry, 35(3), 561-602.

Gordon, J., and Lenhardt, R. A. (2010). Rethinking Work and Citizenship. UCLA Law Review, 55, 1161-1238

Hancox, D. (2012). "The Spanish Robin Hood." The Guardian. London, UK: Guardian News and Media Limited. Retrieved from: http://www.guardian.co.uk/world/2012/aug/15/spanish-robin-hood-sanchez-gordillo

Hoerster, K.D., Mayer, J.A., Gabbard, S., Kronick, R.G., Roesch, S.C., Malcame, V.L., and Zúñiga, M.L. (2011). Impact of Individual, Environmental, and Policy-Level Factors on Health Care Utilization Among U.S. Farmworkers. American Journal of Public Health, 101 (4), 685-692.

Holmes, S. M. (2011). Structural vulnerability and hierarchies of ethnicity and citizenship on the farm. Medical Anthropology, 30(4): 425-446.

Holmes, S. M. (2013). Fresh Fruit, Broken Bodies: Migrant Farmworkers in the United States. Berkeley, CA: University of California Press.

Krause, N., Schrezer, T. and Rugulies, R. (2005). Physical Workload, Work Intesification, and Prevalence of Pain in Low Wage Workers: Results from a Participatory Research Project With Hotel Room Cleaners in Las Vegas. American Journal of Industrial Medicine, 48:326-337.

McCauley, A., Langley, K., Rohlman R. (2006). Studying Health Outcomes in Farmworker Populations Exposed to Pesticides. Environmental Health Perspectives, 114(6):953-960.

Mobed, K., Gold, E.B. and Schenker, M. (1992). Occupational Health Problems among Migrant and Seasonal Farm Workers. Western Journal of Medicine, 157(3), 367-373.

Nissen, B., Angee, A., Weinstein, M. (2008) Immigrant Construction Workers and Health and Safety: The South Florida Experience. Labor Studies Journal, 33(1), 48-62. doi: 10.1177/0160449X07312075

Orrenius, P.M., and Zavodny, M. (2009). Do Immigrants Work In Riskier Jobs?. Demography 46(3), 535-551.

Pranksy, M., Portillo, B., Thackery, L., and Hill-Fotouhi, C. (2002). Occupational Risks and Injuries in Non-Agricultural Immigrant Latino Workers. American Journal of Industrial Medicine, 42:117-123.

Sakala, C. (1987).Migrant and Seasonal Farmworkers in the United States: A Review of Health Hazards, Status, and Policy. International Migration Review, 21(3), 659-87.

Schenker, M. (2008). Work-related injuries among immigrants: a growing global health disparity. Occup Environ Med, 65: 717-718.

Schenker, M.B., and McCurdy, S.A. (1990). Occupational health among migrant and seasonal farmworkers: the specific case of dermatitis. American Journal of Independent Medicine, 18(3), 345-51.

Sears, J. M., Bowman, S.M., Adams, D., and Silverstein, B.A. (2013). Who pays for work-related traumatic injuries? Payer distribution in Washington state by ethnicity, injury severity, and year (1998-2008). Am. J. Ind. Med., 56: 742–754.

Stallones, L., Vela Acosta, M.S., Sample, P., Bigelow, P., and Rosales, M. (2009). Perspectives on safety and health among migrant and seasonal farmworkers in the United States and México: A qualitative field study. Journal of Rural Health, 25(2), 219–225.

Walter, N., Bourgois, P., Loinaz, H.M., and Schillinger, D. (2002). Social context of work injury among undocumented day laborers in San Francisco. Journal of General International Medicine, 17(3), 221-229.

Welch, L., Xiuwen, D., Francoise, C., Carre, R. (2007). "Is the Apparent Decrease in Injury and Illness Rates in Construction the Result of Changes in Reporting?" International Journal of Occupational and Environmental Health 13, no. 1: 39–45.

Welch, L., Hunting, K. and Murawski, J. (2005). Occupational injuries among construction workers treated in a major metropolitan emergency department in the United States. Scandinavian Journal of Work, Environment and Health, 2, 11-21.

Yúñez-Naude, A. (2003). The Dismantling of CONASUPO, a Mexican State Trader in Agriculture. The World Economy, 26, 97-122.

Zhang, S. X. (2012). Trafficking of Migrant Laborers in San Diego County: Looking for a Hidden Population. San Diego, CA: San Diego State University.

Resumen

Salud en el trabajo en ambos lados de la frontera

Camila Gavin Bravo, Troy Araiza Kokinis, Marisela Ortíz, Emily Williams, Guadalupe Arceo y Debra Cornelius

En este capítulo se comparan los problemas de salud en el trabajo entre los residentes de Tlacuitapa con los tlacuitapenses que viven en comunidades satélites en los Estados Unidos. Nos preguntamos, en qué país -Estados Unidos o México-, están más seguros los tlacuitapenses en cuanto a su salud en el trabajo?

Para responder a esta pregunta nos centramos en cuatro indicadores clave: percepción de seguridad de los lugares de trabajo, las lesiones y abusos experimentados, el reporte de los agravios, y la búsqueda de tratamiento médico. De esta forma, construir una imagen completa de la variedad de factores que afectan la salud y la seguridad ocupacional. Argumentamos que el bienestar laboral es mejor para los hombres en México, mientras que es mejor para las mujeres en los Estados Unidos.

En general, los tlacuitapenses experimentan tasas más altas de accidentes en el trabajo en los Estados Unidos (28 por ciento) que en México (14,9 por ciento). Los hombres son más susceptibles a los accidentes de trabajo en los Estados Unidos, ya que mayoritariamente trabajan en la construcción, el sector con el mayor porcentaje de accidentes de trabajo (78,6 por ciento). Las mujeres son un poco más susceptibles a los accidentes de trabajo en Tlacuitapa, como consecuencia de las restringidas oportunidades de empleo disponibles para ellas, lo que las limita en gran parte a la industria de fabricación en los que corren un alto riesgo de lesiones. Tanto en Estados Unidos como en México, los tlacuitapenses tiene en promedio dos lesiones relacionadas con el trabajo durante toda su vida.

Por otra parte, las tasas de acoso laboral son altas para los trabajadores tlacuitapenses en ambos lados de la frontera. Al considerar el género, el 30 por ciento de los hombres y el 38 por ciento de las mujeres en México han sufrido abusos en el lugar de trabajo, en comparación con los Estados Unidos, donde el 35 por ciento de los hombres y el 17 por ciento de las mujeres han sufrido abusos.

El robo de salarios y el abuso verbal son los tipos más comunes de los abusos sufridos por tlacuitapenses en ambos países. Las tasas de robo de salarios aumenta para hombres y mujeres una vez que emigran a Estados Unidos, puede deberse a factores como la barrera del idioma y el estatus migratorio.

Cuando se trata de la percepción de seguridad en el lugar de trabajo, las mujeres en México son quienes más reconocen las condiciones adversas de trabajo, mientras que los hombres que trabajan en los Estados Unidos perciben en mayor número, la preocupación de sus empleadores para no poner en riesgo a los trabajadores. Aún así, son estos hombres quienes sufren el mayor porcentaje de lesiones relacionadas con el trabajo.

Los tlacuitapenses reportan con mayor frecuencia los accidentes de trabajo en Estados Unidos que en México, pero en generla, no informan a las autoridades correspondientes. Noventa y tres por ciento de tlacuitapenses en los Estados Unidos, informaron de su lesión a su empleador, mientras que sólo el 50 por ciento de los de México informó a su empleador.

La mayoría de los trabajadores de Tlacuitapa tanto en México (89 por ciento) como en Estados Unidos (93 por ciento), reciben tratamiento después de una lesión relacionada con el trabajo. Hay muy poca variación en los tipos de tratamiento buscado entre hombres y mujeres en cualquier localidad.

Las pobres condiciones de salud ocupacional han producido una amplia variedad de consecuencias negativas para los tlacuitapenses en ambos lados de la frontera. La educación, la vigilancia al respeto de derechos laborales y la sindicalización de los trabajadores de ambos países, podrían contribuir a mejorar la salud ocupacional de esta población. Por otra parte, en los Estados Unidos, un programa de legalización integral sin duda mejoraría la salud en el trabajo de los migrante.

Sin embargo, creemos que la mala salud ocupacional de los tlacuitapenses, es el resultado de presiones macroestructurales que se aparecen en la producción de un mercado globalizado. Los migrantes se convierten en una clase obrera transnacional, que permite la competitividad en este mercado al ser una mano de obra barata.

Folkloric dancers at Tlacuitapa's annual fiestas.
(Photograph by Risa Farrell)

6 Se Van Feos y Regresan Guapos: Sexuality, Power, and Immigration Policy in Rural Mexico

Allison Van Vooren, Brad Waples, Jaime López, Risa Farrell, Daniel Lepe And Isela Martínez

> *"Se van feos y regresan guapos" (They leave ugly and come back handsome)* —26 year-old female, Tlacuitapa

INTRODUCTION

Dazzling red, blue, green, and purple confetti fills the night air as hundreds of Tlacuitapenses flood the central plaza. Mariachi music and laughter drown out the conversations of young women in stilettos and short dresses who circle the plaza, surrounded by a ring of men. Dressed in checkered shirts and cowboy hats, the men shower their favorite woman in confetti, hoping the attraction is mutual and she will let him walk with her the rest of the night.

For two weeks every January, the rural town of Tlacuitapa, Jalisco, erupts in fiestas honoring their patron saint, the Virgin of Guadalupe. Migrants from the United States return for the celebration and young girls compete for the title of town "queen." The vacationing migrant men enjoy heightened social status and attractiveness to the women of the town, and public displays of courtship on these nights often end in partnerships. Given the limited duration of the fiestas, relationships develop rapidly and can lead to hasty sexual encounters.

The sexual encounters that occur during the fiestas may result in what researchers and public health professionals often cite as "risk behaviors" – individual failures to abide by safe sex practices. Yet, by placing the focus on individual behavior, public health discourse overlooks the macro-social structures that create such vulnerabilities (Holmes 2011). Despite the growing body of socio-cultural literature on the spread of HIV and other sexually transmitted infections (STIs) (Hirsch, 2009, 2002; Ojeda et al., 2012; Parrado and Flippen, 2010; Snyder et al., 2000; Zavriew, 1994), relatively little attention has been given to the structural vulnerability of non-migrant women that is created by U.S. immigration policies.

In examining the ways in which immigration policies established by the United States shape sexuality, we argue for a comprehensive analysis accounting for the social structures that create and facilitate individual risk. Policy plays a critical role in the construction of sexuality in Tlacuitapa, leading us to ask what relationship exists between immigration policies and the risk of HIV transmission?

We argue that U.S. immigration policies of the last several decades, designed to reduce the number of migrants entering the country, have had the unintended consequence of creating an exclusive status among male migrants. This perception of exclusivity imbues migrants with disproportionate power over non-migrant males with whom they interact during the annual fiestas. Furthermore, this power inequality becomes particularly relevant in the negotiation of sexual practices, as women who engage in short-term encounters may be willing to compromise their use of protective measures, including the use of condoms.

By illuminating the factors involved in shaping migrant exclusivity, we avoid limiting this study to a simplistic view of behavioral risk and instead focus on structural vulnerabilities of HIV infection. Refocusing academic discourse surrounding HIV risk towards the underlying socio-political structures allows us to discuss and recommend comprehensive policy measures aimed at reducing STI and HIV-related risk (Holmes, 2011).

MIGRATION FROM TLACUITAPA

Tlacuitapa has a four-generation history of migration to the United States. Initially, migrant flows from Tlacuitapa were relatively unrestricted and circular migration to and from Mexico was common. Despite the termination of the Bracero Program in 1964, Tlacuitapenses continued to migrate at a similar rate (Cornelius, Fitzgerald, and Borger, 2009). With the introduction of the Immigration Reform and Control Act (IRCA) of 1986, a majority of Tlacuitapenses living in the United States at the time became legal residents. In the 2007 MMFRP study of Tlacuitapa, 24 percent of those who had a green card reported obtaining it through IRCA (Vázquez, Luna Gómez, Law, and Valentine, 2009).

However, relatively recent U.S. immigration policies have made undetected migration to the United States more difficult for Tlacuitapenses lacking papers. The 1990s saw the increased militarization of the U.S. border. "Operation Gatekeeper" in San Diego, California and "Operation Rio Grande" in the Rio Grande Valley in Texas were just two of the efforts aimed at reducing illegal entries into the United States (Purcell and Nevins, 2005; Cornelius, 2001, 2008). The implementation of these "prevention through deterrence" policies markedly decreased circular flows of undocumented migration and dramatically increased the cost and dangers of border crossing (Alarcon ,2011; Cornelius, 2001). The attacks of September 11, 2001 prompted further increases in border enforcement, pushing undocumented migrants into more remote and dangerous parts of the border.

The increasingly dangerous nature of clandestine border crossing has been accompanied by the absence of immigration reforms at the national level, leading to a situation in which Mexicans without documentation who might like to migrate north face many difficulties and dangers in attempting to do so. Tlacuitapenses without legal authorization to enter the United States have less and less hope of going north. Indeed, 72 percent of interviewees in our study say U.S. immigration policies over the last five years have made obtaining documents to live or work in the United States more challenging, and 90 percent perceive unauthorized border crossing to be "very dangerous". The added risk involved in crossing and the perception of increased difficulty in obtaining legal residency have reinforced the notion of migrant exclusivity in Tlacuitapa, with those who have legal residency in the United States being seen to have "made it" in the eyes of many Tlacuitapenses.

MIGRATION AND RISK OF HIV

The long history and high rate of migration from Tlacuitapa to the United States make it an excellent case study to examine the health risks associated with such transnational movements. Previous studies have shown that Mexican migrants to the United States are particularly vulnerable to exposure to STIs, including HIV (Organista et al., 1996; Ojeda et al., 2012; Parrado and Flippen, 2010; Hirsch et al., 2002; Brouwer et al., 2006; Sanchez et al., 2004). Migrants are at heightened HIV risk in the United States due to a variety of structural and environmental factors including family separation, poor access to care, male-only living conditions, injection drug use, proximity to sex workers, the potential for multiple concurrent partners, and the prevalence of men who have sex with men (MSM) (Magis-Rodríguez et al., 2009; Zavriew, 1994; Rangel et al., 2006; Hirsch et al., 2009). Areas with the highest prevalence of HIV, including the states of Veracruz and Jalisco as well as Mexico City (CENSIDA, 2012), are also among those with the largest number of migrants to the United States (Magis-Rodríguez et al., 2004). Although migrants as well as non-migrants in Tlacuitapa can be exposed to various STIs, we focus on HIV due to its increasing importance as a public health problem in rural Mexico.

An increasing proportion of female HIV cases in Mexico have been linked to migrant men who became infected while living in the United States and, upon return to Mexico, infect their partner(s) (Rangel et al. 200). This "ruralization of AIDS" is becoming increasingly prevalent throughout Mexico, and is a significant public health concern (Ojeda et al., 2012; Magis-Rodríguez et al., 2009). The movement of men between the United States and Mexico puts non-migrant women in migrant-sending communities at risk for HIV, even though the women have never left their hometown (Hernandez-Rosete, 2008; Zavriew, 1994). In fact, marriage presents the single greatest risk factor for HIV infection among women in rural Mexico (Hirsch et al., 2007). Wives often have reduced negotiation power in regards to condom use because it is seen as an assumption of spousal infidelity (Snyder et al., 2000; Hirsch et al., 2002).

For unmarried women, the focus of our study, gender norms and socially constructed expectations of sexuality often supercede considerations of biological risk, leaving women particularly vulnerable to STI and HIV infection. The hope of meeting and establishing a relationship with a man with migration experience, for some Tlacuitapense women, outweighs the desire to protect themselves from STIs that migrant men may bring back with them from the north.

HIV-RELATED PERCEPTIONS AND PROTECTIVE PRACTICES IN TLACUITAPA

To date, HIV has not been officially documented in Tlacuitapa; private and public health professionals we interviewed said they have yet to see a case of HIV. Further, approximately 92 percent of Talcuitapenses reported never having met a person with HIV. Despite the apparent absence of HIV in Tlacuitapa, most Tlacuitapenses have a strong understanding of how HIV is transmitted: 98 percent of the population recognized that HIV can be transmitted by unprotected sex with someone that carries the virus.

To analyze the unique risk-related behavior during the town's annual fiestas, we stratified the data regarding condom perceptions and usage by migrant men (of any age or marital status) and single non-migrant women under the age of forty. We limited the data analysis in such a way as to address the sexual interactions between migrant men who return for the fiestas and the women who are most prone to interact with these men. When asked whether they were in favor of condom use, 89 percent (N=149) of migrant men and 79 percent of single non-migrant women under the age of 40 (N=24) claimed to be in favor of condom use. As Belén, a 37 year-old Tlacuitapense woman living in Oklahoma City noted, making light of condom use, "no hat, no party!" Generally speaking, then, migrant men and non-migrant women are largely in favor of condom use.

Although these data suggest widespread knowledge about HIV transmission and approval of condom usage, we found a significant gap between beliefs and practices among Tlacuitapenses. Forty-five percent of migrant men reported using condoms infrequently, and 46 percent of migrant men said that they "never" use condoms. Seventy-two percent of non-migrant women used condoms infrequently, and 32 percent reported "never" using condoms. In their most recent sexual encounter, 35 percent of migrant men and 12 percent of non-migrant women reported using a condom.

Why, despite knowledge of transmission of HIV, do non-migrant Tlacuitapense women still engage in risky sexual behavior? Similar inconsistencies have been identified in previous studies (Organista et al., 2004; Hirsch, 2007, 2010; Szasz, 1998,). However, we posit that the construction of what we call "migratory masculinity," which confers elevated status and attraction to migrant men, as well as strict community expectations of female virginity, help to explain the discrepancy between knowledge of HIV risk and the lack of condom use among non-migrant Tlacuitapense women.

MIGRATORY MASCULINITY

In discussing the connection between masculinity and globalization, Connell emphasizes the plurality, fluidity, and hierarchy of masculine identities, arguing that gender hegemony is associated with patterns of trade and communication dominated by the global North (Connell, 1998). Writing with Messerschmidt, Connell has argued that these global structures permit the dominance of certain masculine qualities and behaviors, and serve as models of reference for other males (Connell and Messerschmidt, 2005). This concept of "hegemonic masculinity" is rooted in defined contexts of space and time, and constructed by the actors (men and women) who interact and form a set of relationships in these contexts (Kimmel, 2005; Hirsch et al., 2010).

Studies of masculinity in contemporary Mexico reject the simplicity of "machismo" and instead emphasize the complex negotiation of masculine identities and gendered strategies in the context of varied political, economic, and social conditions (Broughton, 2008; Gutmann, 1998, 2006; Cantú, 2009). In the case of Tlacuitapa, a town with high rates of out-migration, the dynamic construction of hegemonic masculinity is intimately tied to successful migration from Mexico to the United States. As Parrini notes in his study of Mexican migrants from Jalisco, Michacán, and Oaxaca, the male body is transformed throughout the process of migration. In the United States, the migrant body symbolizes otherness and invites discrimination, but upon return to Mexico the body represents success and warrants celebration (Parrini 2007). The perils of border crossing and the difficulty of obtaining documents further reinforce migrant men as a superior and exclusive group with certain social advantages. This establishes migration to the United States as a key element in the construction of hegemonic masculinity in Mexico.

When asked if migrant men have an advantage in meeting women, Martha, a fifty-five year old woman living in Tlacuitapa responded,

> Ah, yes. A man comes with a car and the women think he's a great person because they don't know what's on the other side of the border. People here think that because they live in the United States they have it easy.

Parrini also writes that migrants who return to their hometown justify their journey and distinguish themselves from those who have not migrated by displaying symbols of status and accomplishment. As Broughton notes, this display of material wealth is a strategic gendered practice that proves the virility and courage of migrant men, setting them apart from those who have not migrated north (Broughton 2008). In Tlacuitapa, migrant men who have returned for the fiestas display their status in the form of new trucks, expensive clothes, and fancy cell phones acquired in the United States.

Non-migrant men are well aware of their position in the male status hierarchy of Tlacuitapa. As 17-year-old Israel told us, "there are a lot of migrants coming from [the United States], and they act like, 'well, I come from [the United States] so I can do whatever I want.'" Twenty-five year-old Gerardo concurred:

> [Migrants] come and think that they are above us and that we are below [them] just because we are here. Well, it's because they come from over there. It is more about what they bring than who they are. It is more to say I have nice trucks or something or I have money. According to them it is for that reason, because they come from above.

In addressing migrants as coming "from above," Gerardo acknowledges their geographical place of residence as well as their standing in the social hierarchy of Tlacuitapa. As such, physical objects and possessions mark migrants with the power and mystique of El Norte, embodying a hegemonic migratory masculinity that sets them apart from those who have not made the trip north.

THE ATTRACTION OF MIGRANT MEN

Thus established as superior models of masculinity, migrant men are particularly attractive, and many women in Tlacuitapa see them as desirable partners. Some women identified the economic benefits of partnering with a migrant man. Teresa, a 53-year-old, non-migrant woman living in Tlacuitapa remarked, "[Women] like the young men from the United States more because they think they will have a better life with them."

The success symbols displayed by migrant men translate into female expectations that the men can provide a better life for them through a boost to their economic or social status. This is particularly telling within the context of Martha's comment discussing the perception of non-migrant men as less capable than a migrant man of providing for a family. "Few non-migrant men get married," Martha told us. "Many times it's because they don't have the resources and they can't support a family."

Other women, however, noted a more complex interaction of factors beyond economic, social, and legal resources in describing the attraction to migrant men. Take for instance the observations of Esperanza, a 31-year-old, non-migrant woman living in Tlacuitapa:

> Interviewer: For girls here, what happens if a guy comes back with papers... is he attractive?
> Esperanza: He attracts them, a lot. The whole world will say, "Hey look at that guy, he is handsome." Yes, yes, yes.
> Interviewer: Is it a hope to be with a migrant who arrives from the United States?
> Esperanza: I think that for some young women, yes. I have met both types; there are those that don't. Not because they have papers, not because they are migrants, not because they come from over there. And there are those that say "Hey, he has papers" or "He was born there" or

"He is from outside." And look, throw everything at him.
Simply because he is an outsider.

Reyna, a 26-year-old Tlacuitapense living in Oklahoma City, echoed this
sentiment even more strongly when describing how she met her current
husband. He was a migrant who returned to Tlacuitapa for the annual
fiestas, and, at the time she had never gone to the United States.

> You know, ever since I saw him he was interesting to
> me....He had this I don't know what that called my
> attention. And after that, I met a lot of guys but none
> ever interested me as much as he did.

Beyond the tangible economic aspects, these women identify a more
visceral form of attraction to migrant men. Although the outward
symbols of success and the benefits they appear to promise for women are
present, another level of attraction exists: Migrant men embody a form of
masculinity that makes them particularly attractive to non-migrant women.

During the fiestas, this attraction to migrant men is intensified by the
fleeting nature of their visits, heightening the urgency of women to attract a
migrant partner. Adriana, a 20-year-old, non-migrant woman, explained to
us how she had planned her outfits for each night of the two-week fiestas.
For someone with limited resources, this extensive effort indicates not only
a significant monetary investment, but demonstrates the importance of
attracting a suitable partner during the fiestas, of whom, migrant men hold
the most prestige and desirability.

Given this pressure to find a migrant partner within a restricted time
period, women may accept sexual offers that they would otherwise reject.
When was asked about the brief time migrant men are in town, 25-year-
old Gerardo commented:

> They come and since they are only here a short time,
> they don't ask anything, they just say their name and
> that's it. Here you don't have space or time to get to
> know each other.

Sandra further reinforced this sentiment, mentioning the implications of the presence of visiting migrants during the fiestas.

> It's impressive if they come from there [the United States]. They have this 'I don't know what', and they take advantage of it.... the men who come back expect to have sex.

SOCIAL CONTROL OF SEXUALITY

Previous studies have shown that migrant men conceptualize women from their hometown as either sexual objects for pleasure or stable, unerotic marriage partners (Szasz, 1998; González-López, 2005). For their part, women can strategically use sex as a powerful tool in securing a migrant man. However, in socially conservative Tlacuitapa, pre-marital sex is largely seen as shameful, and a woman who engages in such acts risks jeopardizing her reputation in the town. Women face expectations from their family, the Catholic Church, and community residents to remain a virgin and maintain a reputation of purity (González-López, 2005; Hernández, 2009).

Female virginity is a publicly controlled and mediated value that is especially reinforced by the small population of Tlacuitapa. One particular display of this value is the tradition of marriage in a white dress, signifying to the community that the bride is a virgin. Many interviewees mentioned this symbol as an important public marker of female sexual naiveté. When asked if a girl can get married in a white dress if she's not a virgin, one middle-aged man remarked: "Well, yes, you can go and buy yourself a dress but it weighs on your conscience that you don't deserve to go in white. You're not pure anymore, and you're going to the church to swear by your purity." Nadia reflects on her own experience getting married in Tlacuitapa, noting, "Yes, here you must be dressed in white [for your wedding]. I got married in a white dress, the pride of my family."

Aside from weddings, expectations of purity are equally important in everyday relationships. Community rumor, gossip, and the importance of reputation have concrete effects on personal decisions regarding sexual health. For example, in order to maintain the public image of virginity, women are less likely to access condoms or ask their partners to use such protective measures (Goldenberg, Kessler, and Quezada, 2011; Snyder et al., 2000). Asking for condoms implies previous sexual experience and knowledge and has the potential to undermine a woman's reputation and image of purity in the community. When asked how a town member would react upon seeing a young girl with condoms, Esperanza responded:

> They would say "Oooh that girl's carrying a condom, she must be getting around. There is a lot of gossip here. They say, "Hey, look at that girl, she must be going out with that guy." It's just because the town is so small, you're known everywhere. You aren't allowed to start your love life until you're married. It's wrong to have sex without being married.

This constant vigilance and assumed female sexual nievetë makes condom use and negotiation for women who engage in premarital sex exceedingly difficult. As such, gendered expectations of female purity and sexual innocence mediate intricacies in sexual negotiation during the fiestas.

A strong attraction to migrant men coupled with the desire for social mobility complicates women's behavior in an environment where they are expected to remain chaste. Since migrant men represent an opportunity for economic security and the prospects for a better life, women make themselves sexually available to men despite the social and biological risks. Commenting on the women of Tlacuitapa, a migrant man noted, "Here you can easily get a woman, it's just a matter of if you want to or not." Given this perception of women as replaceable, non-migrant women understand that if they do not satisfy or comply with a migrant men's sexual desires (such as sex without a condom), these men can easily find another woman who will. Thus, for women, the biological risk associated with unprotected sex outweighs the social and economic risk associated with missing the opportunity to establish a relationship with a migrant man. This dynamic not only reinforces gender inequality and shifts the balance of sexual negotiations in favor of men, but also increases women's vulnerability to STI and HIV infection.

As such, sexual health repercussions may be significant for women in Tlacuitapa, especially if the encounter involves a man who has had sexual partners on both sides of the border. Since migrant men are at a much higher risk of contracting HIV in the United States and can transmit the infection to their partners in Mexico, the reduced power that women have in negotiations over sexual practices puts them at high risk for STIs and HIV in Tlacuitapa.

CONCLUSION

Our study explores HIV risk among migrant-men and non-migrant women in the high-migrant sending town of Tlacuitapa. Situating this study in a rural Mexican community with a high rate of migration to the United States allows us to better understand the complex relationship between immigration policy and social constructions of gender as it relates to low rates of condom use and substantial HIV risk.

We find a significant discrepancy between attitudes about condom use and sexual practices and argue that this gap can be explained by the hegemonic masculinity that migrant men embody. This migratory masculinity, established through decades of increasingly tighter U.S. border enforcement that have elevated the social status of migrant men, gives them increased sexual negotiation and leverage in relationships with non-migrant women. This gender inequality underlies and influences non-migrant women's risk for exposure to STIs, including HIV.

Unlike previous studies of migration and STI risk that focus on individual risk factors, we argue for a broadening of the scope to include a critical examination of the role of U.S. immigration policies in shaping sexual practices in migrant-sending communities like Tlacuitapa. As Holmes, Hirsch, and others have argued, STI and HIV risk assessment must reflect the political and cultural structures that produce disparities between knowledge and practice in HIV risk-reduction behavior (Holmes, 2011; Hirsch, 2007). Solely addressing individual risk ignores the broader socio-political factors that create an environment of risk and presents the situation as a behavioral issue, treatable by technical means (Ferguson, 1994). This "rendering technical" places blame on the victim and ultimately worsens and prolongs the problem by allowing structural inequality to continue. We argue that structural vulnerability to STI and HIV transmission in Tlacuitapa is profoundly political and must be addressed to prevent undue public health risk. Thus, we seek to direct attention to the significant implications of restrictive immigration policies for gender dynamics, sexual health, and STI and HIV risk for communities such as Tlacuitapa.

Even as we have looked to critically examine the consequences of migration for the sexual health of Tlacuitapa, many questions and avenues for further research remain. Additional effects of migratory masculinity on gender dynamics would be of particular interest. Is domestic and partner violence changing or being redefined in places like Tlacuitapa? Does increasing media influence, both Mexican and American, valorize migrant men or promote changing perceptions of sexuality? Our study has demonstrated the importance of evaluating how migration can have far-reaching consequences, beyond the strictly economic impacts on migrant-sending and receiving communities, and calls for further attention to other such effects.

REFERENCES

Alarcón, R. (2011). U.S. Immigration Policy and the Mobility of Mexicans (1882-2005). Migraciones Internacionales, 6(1), 185–218.

Alber, M., & Brock, L. (1998). New Relationships Between Territory and State. In D. Spencer and K. Staudt (eds.), The U.S.-Mexico Border: Transcending Divisions, Contesting Identities. Boulder, Colorado: Lynne Rienner Publishers.

Broughton, C. (2008). Migration as Engendered Practice: Mexican Men, Masculinity, and Northward Migration. Gender & Society, 22(5), 568–589. doi:10.1177/0891243208321275

Brouwer, K.C., Strathdee, S.A., Magis-Rodríguez, C., Bravo-García, E., Gayet, C., Patterson, T., Hogg, R.S. (2006). Estimated Numbers of Men and Women Infected with HIV/AIDS in Tijuana, Mexico. Journal of Urban Health, 83(2), 299–307. doi:10.1007/s11524-005-9027-0

Cantú, L., Naples, N., & Vidal-Ortiz, S. (2009). The Sexuality of Migration: Border Crossings and Mexican Immigrant Men. New York: New York University Press.

Castañeda, X., Brindis, C., & Camey, I. C. (2001). Nebulous Margins: Sexuality and Social   Constructions of Risks in Rural Areas of Central Mexico. Culture, Health & Sexuality, 3(2), 203–219.

Centro Nacional para la Prevención y Control del SIDA (CENSIDA). (2009) El VIH/SIDA en México 2009. México, D.F.

Cohen, J.H. (2004). The Culture of Migration in Southern Mexico. University of Texas Press.

Connell, R.W. (1998). Masculinities and Globalization. Men and Masculinities, 1(1), 3–23. doi:10.1177/1097184X98001001001

Connell, R.W., & Messerschmidt, J.W. (2005). Hegemonic Masculinity Rethinking the Concept. Gender & Society, 19(6), 829–859. doi:10.1177/0891243205278639

Cornelius, W. A. (1992). From Sojourners to Settlers: The Changing Profile of Mexican Migration to the United States. In J. Bustamante, R. Hinojosa, & C. Reynolds (eds.), Mexico-U.S. Relations: Labor Market Integration. Stanford , CA: Stanford University Press.

Cornelius, W.A., Fitzgerald, D., Borger, S.C., eds. (2009) Four Generations of Norteños: New Research from the Cradle of Mexican Migration. La Jolla, CA and Boulder, CO: Center for Comparative Immigration Studies, University of California, San Diego, and Lynne Rienner Publishers.

Cornelius, W.A., Borger, S., Sawyer, A., Keyes, D., Appleby, C., Parks, K., Lozada, G., Hicken, J. (2008). Controlling Unauthorized Immigration from Mexico: The Failure of "Prevention through Deterrence" and the Need for Comprehensive Reform. Washington, DC: Immigration Policy Center.

Donaldson, M. (1993). What is hegemonic masculinity? Theory and Society, 22, 643–657.

Ferguson, J. (1990). The Anti-Politics Machine: "Development", Depoliticization, and Bureaucratic Power in Lesotho. New York and Cambridge: Cambridge University Press.

Goldenberg, S., Kessler, K.,& Quesada, L. (2011). Contraceptive Use in a Community of International Migration. In D.S. Fitzgerald, et al. (eds.), Recession Without Borders: Mexican Migrants Confront the Economic Downturn (pp. 132–152). La Jolla, CA: Center for Comparative Immigration Studies, University of California-San Diego.

González-López, G. (2005). Erotic Journeys: Mexican Immigrants and Their Sex Lives. Berkeley, CA: University of California Press.

Gudelia Rangel, M., Martínez-Donate, A.P., Hovell, M.F., Santibáñez, J., Sipan, C.L., & Izazola-Licea, J.A. (2006a). Prevalence of risk factors for HIV infection among Mexican migrants and immigrants: probability survey in the northern border of Mexico. Salud Pública de México, 48(1), 3–12. doi:10.1590/S0036-36342006000100003

Gutmann, M.C. (1998). El Machismo. In T. Valdés & J. Olavarría (eds.), Masculinidades y equidad de género en América Latina. Santiago, Chile: FLASCO.

Gutmann, M.C. (2006). The Meanings of Macho: Being a Man in Mexico City. Berkeley, CA: University of California Press.

Hanson, G. (2009). The Economics and Policy of Illegal Immigration in the United States. Washington, DC: Migration Policy Institute. Retrieved from https://www.migrationpolicy.org/pubs/Hanson-Dec09.pdf

Harvey, S.M., Beckman, L.J., Browner, C.H., & Sherman, C.A. (2002). Relationship power, decision making, and sexual relations: An exploratory study with couples of Mexican origin. Journal of Sex Research, 39(4), 284–291. doi:10.1080/00224490209552152

Herdt, G., & Lindenbaum, S. (n.d.). The Time of AIDS: Social Analysis, Theory, and Method. United Kingdom: SAGE Publications.

Hernández, O.M. (2009). Descobijando a los hombres: Masculinidades y relaciones de género en Cd. Victoria. Tamaulipas, México: Universidad Autónoma de Tamaulipas.

Hernández-Rosete, D., Maya García, O., Bernal, E., Castañeda, X., & Lemp, G. (2008). Migration and ruralization of AIDS: reports on vulnerability of indigenous communities in Mexico. Revista de Saúde Pública, 42(1), 131–138. doi:10.1590/S0034-89102008000100017

Herrera, A.A. (1998). Virginity in Mexico: The role of competing discourses of sexuality in personal experience. Reproductive Health Matters, 6(12), 105–115. doi:10.1016/S0968-8080(98)90013-1

Hesbert, B.C. (2012). Liberalismo, comunitarismo e inmigración. Desacatos, 39, 105–122.

Hicken, J., Fishbein, J., & Lisle, J. (2011). U.S. Border Enforcement: The Limits of Physical and Remote Deterrence of Unauthorized Migration. In D. S. Fitzgerald, et al. (eds.), Recession Without Borders: Mexican Migrants Confront the Economic Downturn (pp. 132–152). La Jolla, CA: Center for Comparative Immigration Studies, University of California-San Diego.

Hirsch, J.S., Higgins, J., Bentley, M.E., & Nathanson, C.A. (2002). The Social Constructions of Sexuality: Marital Infidelity and Sexually Transmitted Disease–HIV Risk in a Mexican Migrant Community. American Journal of Public Health, 92(8), 1227–1237.

Hirsch, J.S., Muñoz-Laboy, M., Nyhus, C.M., Yount, K.M., & Bauermeister, J.A. (2009). They   "Miss More Than Anything Their Normal Life Back Home": Masculinity and Extramarital Sex Among Mexican Migrants in Atlanta. Perspectives on Sexual and Reproductive Health, 41(1), 23–32. doi:10.1363/4102309

Hirsch, J. S., Smith, D. J., Nathanson, C.A., & Phinney, H.M. (2010). The Secret: Love, Marriage, and HIV. Nashville, TN: Vanderbilt University Press.

Hirsch, J. S., Meneses, S., Thompson, B., Negroni, M., Pekcastre, B. & del Rio, C. (2007). The Inevitability of Infidelity: Sexual Reputation, Social Geographies, and Marital HIV Risk in Rural Mexico. American Journal of Public Health, 97(6).

Holmes, S.M. (2011). Structural Vulnerability and Hierarchies of Ethnicity and Citizenship on the Farm. Medical Anthropology, 30(4), 425–449. doi:10.1080/01459740.2011.576728

Hondagneu-Sotelo, P. (1994). Gendered Transitions: The Mexican Experience of Immigration. Berkeley. CA: University of California Press.

Jarvis, J., Ponce, A., Rodríguez, S., & Garcia, L.C. (2009). The Dynamics of Migration: Who Migrates? Who Settles Abroad? In W.A. Cornelius, D.S. Fitzgerald, & S. Borger. (eds.), Four Generations of Norteños: New Research from the Cradle of Mexican Migration. San Diego, CA and Boulder, CO: Center for Comparative Immigration Studies at the University of California, San Diego, and Lynne Rienner Publishers.

Kanaiaupuni, S. M. (2000). Reframing the Migration Question: An Analysis of Men, Women, and Gender in Mexico. Social Forces, 78(4), 1311–1347. doi:10.1093/sf/78.4.1311

Kimmel, M. S., Hearn, J., & Connell, R. (2005). Handbook of Studies on Men and Masculinities. Beverly Hills, CA: SAGE Publications.

Magis-Rodríguez, C., Lemp, G., Hernández, M.T., Sánchez, M.A., Estrada, F.

Bravo-García, E. (2009). Going North: Mexican Migrants and Their Vulnerability to HIV. JAIDS: Journal of Acquired Immune Deficiency Syndromes, 51(Supplement 1), S21–S25. doi:10.1097/QAI.0b013e3181a26433

Magis-Rodríguez, C. (n.d.). Migration and AIDS in Mexico: An Overview Based on Recent Evidence. Journal of Acquired Immune Deficiency Syndromes. Retrieved from http://journals.lww.com/jaids/Fulltext/2004/11014/Migration_and_AIDS_in_Mexico__An_Overview_Based_on.3.aspx

Melhuus, M., & Stølen, K A. (1996). Machos, Mistresses and Madonnas: Contesting the Power of Latin American Gender Imagery. New York and London: Verso.

Ojeda, V.D., Burgos, J.L., Hiller, S.P., Lozada, R., Rangel, G., Vera, A., Magis-Rodriguez, C. (2012). Circular migration by Mexican female sex workers who are injection drug users: implications for HIV in Mexican sending communities. Journal of Immigrant and Minority Health, 14(1), 107–115. doi:10.1007/s10903-011-9512-3

Organista, K.C., Organista, P.B., Garcia de Alba, J.E., Castillo Moran, M.A. &Carrillo, H. (1996). AIDS and Condom-Related Knowledge, Beliefs, and Behaviors in Mexican Migrant Laborers. Hispanic Journal of Behavioral Sciences, 18(3), 392–406. doi:10.1177/07399863960183008

Ortner, S.B., & Whitehead, H. (1981). Sexual Meanings: The Cultural Construction of Gender and Sexuality. New York and Cambridge: Cambridge University Press.

Parrado, E.A., & Flippen, C.A. (2010). Migration and Sexuality: A Comparison of Mexicans in Sending and Receiving Communities. Journal of Social Issues, 66(1), 175–195. doi:10.1111/j.1540-4560.2009.01639.x

Parrini, R., Castañeda, X., Magis, C., Ruiz, J., & Lemp, G. (2007). Migrant bodies: Corporality, sexuality, and power among Mexican migrant men. Sexuality Research & Social Policy, 4(3), 62–73. doi:10.1525/srsp.2007.4.3.62

Purcell, M., & Nevins, J. (2005). Pushing the boundary: state restructuring, state theory, and the case of U.S.–Mexico border enforcement in the 1990s. Political Geography, 24(2), 211–235. doi:10.1016/j.polgeo.2004.09.015

Rangel, G. M., Martínez-Donate, A.P., Hovell, M.F., Santibáñez, J., Sipan, C.L., & Izazola-Licea, J.A. (2006). Prevalence of risk factors for HIV infection among Mexican migrants and immigrants: probability survey in the northern border of Mexico. Salud Pública de México, 48(1), 3–12. doi:10.1590/S0036-36342006000100003

Rosas, C. (2008). Varones al son de la migración: Migración internacional y masculinidades de Veracruz a Chicago. México, DF: El Colegio de México.

Sadowski-Smith, C. (2002). Globalization on the Line: Culture, Capital, and Citizenship at U.S. Borders. New York: Palgrave.

Sanchez, M.A., Hernández, M.T., Hanson, J. E., Vera, A., Magis-Rodríguez, C., Ruiz, J. D., Lemp, G.F. (2012). The Effect of Migration on HIV High-Risk Behaviors Among Mexican Migrants. JAIDS: Journal of Acquired Immune Deficiency Syndromes, 61(5), 610–617. doi:10.1097/QAI.0b013e318273b651

Segura, D.A., & Zavella, P. (2008). Introduction: Gendered Borderlands. Gender and Society, 22(5), 537–544. doi:10.2307/27821676

Sisco, J., & Hicken, J. (2009). Is U.S. Border Enforcement Working? In W.A.Cornelius, D.S. Fitzgerald, & S. Borger. (eds.), Four Generations of Norteños: New Research from the Cradle of Mexican Migration. San Diego, CA: Center for Comparative Immigration Studies at the University of California, San Diego.

Smith, R.C. (2006). Mexican New York: Transnational Live of New Immigrants. Berkeley and   Los Angeles, CA: University of California Press.

Snyder, V., Acevedo, A., Díaz-Pérez M.J. & Saldívar-Garduño, A. (2000). Understanding The Sexuality of Mexican-Born Women and Their Risk for HIV/AIDS. Psychology of Women Quarterly, 24(1), 100–109. doi:10.1111/j.1471-6402.2000.tb01026.x

Staudt, K. & Spencer, D. (1998). The View from the Frontier: Theoretical Perspectives Undisciplined. In D. Spencer and K. Staudt (eds.), The U.S.-Mexico Border: Transcending Divisions, Contesting Identities. Boulder, Colorado: Lynne Rienner Publishers.

Strathdee S.A. & Magis-Rodriguez, C. (2008). Mexico's evolving hiv epidemic. Journal of the American Medical Association (5), 571–573. doi:10.1001/jama.300.5.571

Szasz, I. (1998). Masculine identity and the meanings of sexuality: A review of research in Mexico. Reproductive Health Matters, 6(12), 97–104. doi:10.1016 S0968-8080(98)90012-X

Szurmuk M, McKee R. (2009). Diccionario de estudios culturales latinoamericanos. México D.F.: Siglo XXI Editores, Instituto Mora.

Vázquez, L., Luna Gómez, M., Law, E., & Valentine, K. (2009). Jumping The Legal Hurdles: Getting Green Cards, Visas, and U.S. Citizenship. In W.A. Cornelius, D.S. Fitzgerald, & S. Borger. (eds.), Four Generations of Norteños: New Research from the Cradle of Mexican Migration. San Diego, CA: Center for Comparative Immigration Studies at the University of California, San Diego.

Viadro, C.I., & Earp, J.A.L. (2000). The sexual behavior of married Mexican immigrant men in North Carolina. Social Science & Medicine, 50(5), 723–735. doi:10.1016/S0277-9536(99)00305-6

Zavriew, L. (1994). Bringing HIV back to the villages. WorldAIDS, (35), 6.

Resumen

Sexualidad, poder, y la política de inmigración en México rural

Allison Van Vooren, Brad Waples, Jaime López,
Risa Farrell, Daniel Lepe And Isela Martínez

Cada año, durante las primeras dos semanas de enero, los migrantes de Tlacuitapa regresan a su pueblo natal para las fiestas anuales en las que celebran a la Virgen de Guadalupe. Este breve periodo de reunificación trae consigo una abundancia de hombres que trabajan en los Estados Unidos la mayor parte del año y se vuelve un tiempo de noviazgos intensificados entre los jóvenes del pueblo. Citando datos cuantitativos sobre el uso del condón y entrevistas cualitativas con Tlacuitapenses, este estudio encontró que las relaciones sexuales durante las fiestas pueden aumentar el riesgo de transmisión de VIH y otras infecciones de transmisión sexual (ITS) en la comunidad de Tlacuitapa.

Nuestros resultados parecen indicar la presencia de lo que los investigadores y los profesionales de salud pública suelen llamar "conductas de riesgo" -- comportamientos individuales que aumentan el riesgo de contraer enfermedades-- tal como puede ser no practicar el sexo seguro. Por el contrario, se argumenta que las estructuras macro-sociales relacionadas con las políticas de migración y la dinámica de género construye la vulnerabilidad de las mujeres no-migrantes en Tlacuitapa.

Específicamente, sostenemos que las políticas restrictivas de inmigración de EEUU y la militarización de la frontera entre México y Estados Unidos ha creado un nuevo grupo de Tlacuitapenses 'exitosos'. Esta situación exclusiva modifica la definición de la masculinidad hegemónica-- aquí denominada "masculinidad migratoria" -- y valora a los migrantes que regresan al pueblo, haciéndoles especialmente atractivos ante las mujeres que se quedan. Esta percepción de exclusividad y éxito empapa a los migrantes de un poder desproporcionado sobre las mujeres que no migran de Tlacuitapa, con las que interactúan durante las fiestas anuales. Esta desigualdad de poder se vuelve particularmente relevante en la negociación de prácticas sexuales, ya que las mujeres que participan en los encuentros de corto plazo pueden estar dispuestas a hacer concesiones en el uso de medidas de protección, incluyendo el uso del condón.

Nuestros datos cuantitativos demuestran una discrepancia entre el conocimiento de los modos de transmisión de las ITS y el comportamiento para protegerse de la transmisión. El 89 por ciento (N=149) de los hombres migrantes y el 79 por ciento (N=24) de las mujeres no migrantes, solteras, y menores de 40 años reportaron estar a favor del uso del preservativo. Esto contrasta con el uso del condón reportado: 45 por ciento de los hombres migrantes reportaron haber usado preservativos con poca frecuencia y el 46 por ciento de los hombres migrantes dijo que nunca utiliza preservativos. Setenta y dos por ciento de las mujeres no migrantes dijo que usa condones con poca frecuencia, y el 32 por ciento informó que nunca usa condones. En su encuentro sexual más reciente, el 35 por ciento de los hombres migrantes y el 12 por ciento de las mujeres no migrantes reportaron haber usado un condón.

Argumentamos que la construcción de lo que llamamos "la masculinidad migratoria", así como estrictas expectativas de la comunidad acerca de la virginidad femenina ayudan a explicar la discrepancia entre el conocimiento de los riesgos del VIH y la falta del uso del condón entre las mujeres no migrantes de Tlacuitapa. Algunas mujeres identificaron beneficios económicos a la asociación con un hombre migrante, mientras otras señalaron una forma de atracción más ambigua y visceral. Una mujer no migrante de cincuenta y tres años y viviendo en Tlacuitapa comentó, "a las mujeres les gustan los muchachos de los Estados Unidos porque piensan que van a tener una vida mejor con ellos". Hablando del día cuando conoció a su marido durante las fiestas, otra Tlacuitapense de veintiséis años dijo: "sabes que, desde que lo vi fue interesante para mí. Él tenía ese no sé qué que me llamó la atención". Así, el deseo de asociarse con un hombre migrante durante el corto tiempo de las fiestas aumenta la probabilidad de que las mujeres puedan tomar decisiones apresuradas que las ponen en riesgo de contraer VIH u otra ITS.

Junto con el aumento de estatus y poder de los hombres migrantes, el valor social y la expectativa feminina de ser una mujer virgen y pura antes del matrimonio, también promovido por el rumor, el 'chisme', y la reputación pública, se espera que las mujeres sean inocentes e ignorantes acerca de temas de sexualidad, tal como la prevención de ITS. Por ejemplo, pedir condones implica experiencia sexual y puede socavar la reputación de una mujer y su imagen de pureza ante su comunidad.

Por lo tanto, esta situación de poder sexual desequilibrada entre los hombres migrantes y las mujeres no migrantes en Tlacuitapa restringe el acceso y el uso de condones, aumentando la vulnerabilidad al VIH y las ITS en Tlacuitapa.

RETURN MIGRATION, HEALTH, AND SEXUALITY
IN A TRANSNATIONAL MEXICAN COMMUNITY

MIGRACIÓN DE RETORNO, SALUD Y SEXUALIDAD
EN UNA COMUNIDAD MEXICANA TRANSNACIONAL

Se terminó de imprimir
en los talleres gráficos
de Prometeo Editores, S.A. de C.V.
Calle Libertad No. 1457
44160, Guadalajara, Jalisco
Tel. 01 (33) 3826-2726

Su tiraje consta de 500 ejemplares

Impreso en México Printed in Mexico